Harmless as Doves

Witnessing for Peace in Vietnam

Mary Sue H. Rosenberger

BRETHREN PRESS
Elgin, Illinois

Harmless as Doves
Witnessing for Peace in Vietnam

Copyright © 1988 by Mary Sue H. Rosenberger

BRETHREN PRESS, 1451 Dundee Avenue, Elgin, IL 60120

Cover design by Kathy Kline Miller

Permission to reprint news excerpts was given by Newsweek, Inc., 444 Madison Avenue, New York, NY 11022

Library of Congress Cataloging-in-Publication Data

Rosenberger, Mary Sue H., 1940-
    Harmless as doves: witnessing for peace in Vietnam / Mary Sue H. Rosenberger.
        p.   cm.
    ISBN 0-87178-345-2
    1. Vietnamese Conflict, 1961-1975—War work—Churches. 2. Vietnamese Conflict, 1961-1975—Personal narratives, American. 3. Rosenberger, Mary Sue H., 1940-. I. Title.
DS559.63.R67 1988
959.704' 37—dc 19   88-39526
[B]   CIP

Manufactured in the United States of America

*To those who didn't come back
and
to those who did come back
and can never be the same.*

Contents

1

In Training

Newsweek
April 11, 1966

You'll Need To Know This If You're In Vietnam

They pile off the buses in groups of 30 and 40, motley assortments carrying overnight bags, wearing slacks and loafers, denims and sneakers, long hair and short. They shuffle nervously at the unloading dock, joking too loudly, and they have in common the gangling robustness of youth and one other thing: the glazed, impaled, confused and resigned look of the raw citizen-soldier about to plunge into the fabled terrors of basic Army training.

A map of Vietnam is posted in nearly every office. Many cadremen are veterans of the fighting. "You'll need to know this if you're in Vietnam," is a common preface to a lecture on any subject. One sergeant shows his new men a picture of a youngster who nodded his way through basic at Fort Wood last year; he then shows a clipping about the youth's death in Vietnam. Platoon Sgt. Emery Mortensen tells his trainees to set their M-14 sights by listening to the clicks rather than by looking at the numbers. "What are you going to do in Vietnam at night?" he asks. "You going to shine a flashlight on it and get your head blown off?". . . .

February 13, 1966
BVS Training Center
New Windsor, Maryland

Dear Friends,

These past six weeks since I have seen any of you have passed very quickly. So quickly, in fact, that I have not been able to find time in a busy schedule of new activities to write to any of you. It may take me several days to get that situation remedied but I shall try to explain to you in this document some of what I am doing and why. As this same letter will be coming to so many of you who knew me in different times, places, and contexts and, hence, knew different sides of me, I guess I'd better start from the beginning.

I am now participating in the Brethren Volunteer Service program (BVS) which is a program sponsored by the Church of the Brethren. Persons of all ages—but, for the most part, young—volunteer one or two years of their time through BVS to serve in areas of human need, helping to relieve suffering. Service is performed in many areas around the world where the Church of the Brethren has established projects or can cooperate with other agencies.

The first two months of our time in BVS is spent in training as a unit. We don't study the languages, customs, or religions of the countries to which we will be going or anything like that. In fact, most of us don't even know where we will be going until the next to the last week of our eight weeks' training. We don't even study specific skills which we might be called upon to use on project, except such things as recreation, crafts leadership, and public speaking.

We come into this experience armed with many different skills, backgrounds, and educational levels. The minimum requirements for BVS are to be at least eighteen years of age, to have a high school diploma, and a sincere desire to serve within a Christian context. So, the purpose of this training period seemed rather vague even to me and I had been hearing about the program for years before I entered it. But I'm beginning to realize that it takes some training to prepare the average self-centered, materialistic American youth to serve others. We're being prepared for work that is hard, physical, often dirty, but loving service. The recipients of that service may be unlovable (and often unloving) brothers or sisters we have never seen in a place we've never heard of before but that is far from home. And we'll do it all for only $10 a month plus room and board! It takes training to get prepared for that!

Our training unit is a very interesting assembly of people. We are seven girls and thirty-one fellows from about twelve different states, France, England, and Indonesia. We include a variety of religious perspectives: one Catholic, three Quakers, one humanitarian, one atheist, several cynics and skeptics, one vegetarian, two who come from community living situations (such as Bruderhof) and several very conservative, straight-line Brethren, and members of other Protestant denominations. Our ages vary from nineteen to twenty-nine and our educational backgrounds range from high school to graduate school. The unit includes one married couple; the rest of us are single.

Let me describe a typical day's schedule for this assortment of wonderful people. Four hours of our day are spent in processing clothing which has been collected by the relief organizations of the Church of the Brethren and the Lutheran churches. We help sort, pack, bale, and load this clothing for shipment to areas of need. Two hours of the day are spent in class with a guest leader in a presentation and discussion of the topic of the week, some area of Christian concern in today's world. That takes care of an eight hour day, but we're not done yet!

Monday evening from seven till about nine p.m. we have unit meeting to care for the business of living together. Tuesday and Thursday evenings we have informally structured discussion groups for two hours in order to get to know ourselves and each other better. Learning to get along with each other helps us begin to develop the abilities to relate to the people we will be serving. It's here that some of us begin to see why eight weeks of training are so important. As hard a time as some of us have in understanding each other, it's going to be harder yet learning to understand the people we go out to serve.

Wednesday night we have a special presentation by the guest leader of the week and Friday evenings are left free for fun times planned by the unit. Weekends are used to good advantage, too. We use them to get some practical experience in service with its blessings and pitfalls. For example, the first week we concentrated on getting oriented to the

BVS program, its goals and purposes: we spent the following Saturday in three different institutions close around the Center just doing general maintenance type work such as painting, fixing, and cleaning. We also had a series of psychological tests that weekend which taught some of us some very interesting things about ourselves when they were interpreted!

The second week's theme was "The Meaning of Persons." The weekend following, we divided into three groups and went to Philadelphia and York, Pennsylvania, and Washington, D.C. for weekend work camp experiences in community centers and settlement houses in the inner cities. I went to York and, in spite of having my wallet stolen (the second time in two months!), I had a wonderful time. We did some cleaning and painting, and built a set of bookshelves, too. On Sunday morning I attended a Friends' meeting. I was impressed by the simplicity and closeness of the group and the challenge and sincerity of their worship. I came away feeling that I had discovered a whole new dimension to faith.

The theme of the third week was "Peace Study." We spent the week exploring our own convictions on peace and studying the teachings of the scriptures and the Church of the Brethren on peace and nonviolence.

On Saturday, the entire unit divided into two groups and went to two nearby communities for "Operation Knock-knock." In pairs we went from door to door in town asking for work that we could do for people in or around their homes—such as raking leaves, washing dishes, cleaning basements, washing cars—for free, of course. Four of us were fortunate enough to find four full hours of work at the sixth house where we stopped. So we were occupied for the rest of the morning. Others of the group didn't fare so well. Several were picked up by the police and spent forty-five minutes trying to explain to the police chief what they were doing! It was difficult for me to go door to door trying to give away my help, I'm not sure how I would react if I were on the receiving end of such helpfulness. I'd no doubt think, as many of those people did, that we were out of our minds—but it was fun!

The fourth week was "Practice Project." Each of us was assigned to an institution, agency, or organization providing social services in which our help could be used in some capacity during the week. This week was to serve as a chance to practice the skills, attitudes, and qualities which we will need on our permanent project. I went to a home for the aged operated by the Church of the Brethren near Gettysburg, Pennsylvania. Although they have a nursing shortage, I spent the week just visiting some of the residents and learning to know them. I made some very good friends during the week. I came away feeling even more strongly how much people of every age, condition, and location need love, acceptance, and appreciation.

The weekend after the fourth week was free; however, we had received an invitation from a church in the area to come and conduct their Sunday service and present the BVS program. Guess who got volunteered into giving half of the sermon? You guessed it—me! Nature, however, didn't cooperate. Saturday afternoon, as we returned from practice project, it was snowing. By Saturday night we were snowbound and completely isolated from the outside world by drifts on all of the roads, some up to twenty feet high. Of course we couldn't get to church on Sunday morning (an example of answered prayer?) but worse yet, there were a hundred guests here at the center for a conference. They were snowbound, too, and couldn't get home.

We spent the day Sunday playing in the snow like children, sledding, and jumping into the huge drifts where we could completely disappear from sight. Sunday afternoon, on very short notice, we planned a worship service for the Center community, the unit, and the snowbound guests. It proved to be delightful. Afterwards, some of us from the BVS unit gathered in the lounge and started singing to thaw ourselves out. We ended up with a group of about fifty people for several hours of singing, laughing, and guitar playing. Many of our snowbound guests left us feeling much less homesick and downhearted.

Since 1954, the Mennonite Central Committee has had service workers in South Vietnam. Several other church and religious groups, planning new programs in refugee relief in the country have decided to cooperate with the Mennonites rather than found separate programs. Thus, the Mennonite Central Committee and Church World Service, the service arm of the National Council of Churches of Christ in the USA, are planning to work together in an expanded ministry in Vietnam. They call it the Vietnam Christian Service program (VNCS).

Forty-five people is their goal for this year. They are planning to open community development, medical, and material aid projects in six areas including Saigon, Pleiku, NhaTrang, Danang, and Hue. This cooperative program will serve as the channel through which other church service organizations, like BVS, can contribute qualified people to this field of service.

That was what my interview was all about. The minimum term is usually two or three years. But, because of the nature of the situation there and the stress under which I'm sure we would be working, I made a one year term the condition under which I felt I could go. I simply do not know if, emotionally, I could stand the prospect of spending longer than one year in such a situation. I would, of course, stay longer if I found that the working conditions were tolerable for me. As things look now I will be going for that one year term whenever my application can be processed and travel arrangements can be made.

I view the opportunity with mixed feelings, of course. For one thing, I'm scared. The news media make Vietnam sound like a dangerous place to be. I have never known either war or Communism first hand and so I am very frightened of the unknown. For another thing, I don't know word one of either French or Vietnamese. I can't imagine spending a year unable to talk!

But I am also eager; eager for the challenge of putting Christian-American concern for the Vietnamese people into action without guns and killing. I'm eager to put my hands where so many of our words have been. Human need for care, love, peace, and a responsibility for a brother or sister's need I have known first hand. I'm eager for the challenge of these things I know.

Jesus said once that his followers were to be "wise as serpents and harmless as doves." I'm not sure if this is a wise decision. But, to be willing to be "harmless as doves" in Vietnam at this time seems to me to be a faithful, though frightening, response to his teachings.

The decision is still somewhat tentative and I await definite information but my word has been given. I'm willing to try to be God's dove in Vietnam if that's what is asked of me. Just this week I came across a prayer of Dag Hammersköld's which means so much to me in these days: "For what has been, thanks. For what shall be, yes."

The snow and the trip to New York made an especially busy week so it was almost over before I knew it was here. The theme was "Understanding our World." The following weekend we spent all of Saturday touring our nation's capitol which is only about a two hour's drive from here. Sunday morning's prayer went unanswered and I had to give the sermon which had been snowed out the week before. I may not be a good nurse but I shall always be able to console myself when the going gets rough that I'd be an even worse preacher!

Last week, the sixth, the theme for our study was "Basic Beliefs." With the aforementioned religious differences, you can just guess how hot the discussions got at times. It's a good thing that God's existence doesn't depend upon our debate of the issue because the Creator would surely have been mighty confused last week!

The past weekend was also a pleasant one. Individually or in pairs we were all invited out to spend two days living in various homes of the community. We helped with household or farm chores, played with the children, stuffed ourselves with good home cooking and just generally made ourselves at home. How wonderful it was to be in a real, for-sure living room for a change.

This week is assignment week. Through a series of interviews, tentative project assignments are made and we learn where we will probably be spending the next year or two of service. It's very exciting and anticipation runs high as you may well imagine. Possibilities range from truck driving to social work, from occupational therapy to teaching in any one of thirty-three states and eight foreign countries. This weekend we are split into four groups and go out as deputation teams to nearby churches to interpret the BVS program. After all, it is the churches who are supporting us. In most cases we are responsible for a Saturday night program, Sunday morning Sunday School and church service. All of that requires a good bit of planning.

Next week's theme is "Christian Social Change—Problems in Service." Then, after a two day retreat at Camp Woodbrook and our final communion service, we're on our way!

You probably all have eyestrain by now from reading this document. But in addition to being a letter to you, this is serving as my diary. I shall, for both of these reasons, try very hard to get some news out by this method every month or so. Of course I would love to hear from any and all of you when and if possible but I know that you are busy, too.

Until next time you will be much in my thoughts.

March 15, 1966
Church of the Brethren headquarters
Elgin, Illinois

Dear Family,

Well, we've been involved in our last conference for awhile, and, in about an hour, we're on our way to San Francisco. I sit here in the TWA terminal eager and scared, but mostly disbelieving! These three days here have been spiritually strengthening and I am impressed by the sincere concern of the people who are sending us out. Yes, I'm scared but love and support from other people make it bearable.

2

In Travel

Newsweek
May 16, 1966

Birmingham—Borderline Case

It was Saturday morning, the 30th of April, when elements of the
U.S. First Infantry Division ("The Big Red One") moved northward
along the Cai Bac River on the border between South Vietnam and
Cambodia. As the GI's hacked their way through the dense jungle
underbrush near the tiny village of Lo Go . . . they suddenly ran into
heavy fire. There was a brief skirmish, then a heavy barrage of mortar and automatic-weapons fire pounded in on the Americans from
the west bank of the river—across the border in Cambodia. The
U.S. troops answered with heavy artillery, pouring round after round
across the Cai Bac until the hostile fire was stilled.

The incident, the first in the Vietnam war in which the U.S.
openly admitted firing artillery into neighboring Cambodia, was
part of a massive sweep through critical Tay Ninh Province, an
operation code-named Birmingham. It was also the most dramatic
event of a week that saw an end come to the month-long lull in the
ground war in South Vietnam.

In another major operation called Davy Crockett, units of the
First Cavalry Division (Airmobile), backed up by South Vietnamese
troops, landed in three places last Wednesday in the fertile farming
land north of the city of Bong Son, 280 miles northeast of Saigon.
After four days of fierce fighting, "friendly casualties" were described as light, while 416 of the enemy lay dead and over 500 suspected Viet Cong were captured.

But if Davy Crockett was a most successful example of how to
kill Viet Cong, it was Operation Birmingham, on the Cambodian

border, that was strategically the most significant of the week. Carried out by 15,000 U.S. and Vietnamese troops, its major objective was to sweep through Tay Ninh Province, disrupt the infiltration route from the north and destroy the staging areas the Viet Cong might use if they launch the much anticipated offensive this month after the monsoon rains begin to fall.

March 16, 1966
Honolulu, Hawaii

Dear Folks,

Just a quick note here from Honolulu while I can still use U.S. postage. I put my visa picture in for laughs. At the Mennonite headquarters, they have a saying, "If you look like your passport picture, you needed the trip for your health!" I obviously needed the trip very badly!

One of the pieces of mail which you re-addressed and forwarded was a letter from some sort of "crank." He enclosed a copy of the Dayton Daily News interview with me and marked on it "God pity you." On some of the enclosed propaganda (one of which was entitled "How red is the National Council of Churches?"), he had written "Why go to Vietnam? Your own white sisters here at home need you." At first it concerned me thinking that perhaps people with such attitudes had been bothering you at home. But one of my traveling companions reminded me, "Breathes there a man with soul so dead he never yet has been called a Red?" Then I began to think it was funny!

Must go catch a plane to Hong Kong!

March 18, 1966
Hong Kong

Dear Folks,

Well, we're finally in Hong Kong. You can see on a map that Hong Kong is quite a long way from Chicago where we started three days ago. What an exciting three days, and more to come. There's so much to tell I hardly know where to start.

Our days in Chicago were very pleasant and would have been restful if I had been sensible and gone to bed at a reasonable time. With so many old friends to visit, I didn't, of course. We left Chicago Tuesday a.m. in a brisk cool wind but San Francisco was balmy and warm three hours later. The Rockies and the Continental Divide are beautiful from the air on a clear day.

Another VNCS volunteer, Barbara Stallwood, met us in San Francisco but decided to take a later flight to Honolulu. So the three of us, Bill Herod, Rutus Petre, and I, went on ahead.

Hawaii is unbelievably beautiful from the air and Honolulu, at least, is also gorgeous from the ground. The climate is superb. Tropical vegetation is everywhere. Informality is the word in dress, and Oriental influence is evident in architecture. Our hotel, the Pagoda, was quite nice except for hard beds and we really splurged for dinner our one night in town. We ate at the Pagoda floating restaurant in the center of a large pond which is full of huge, beautifully colored carp. The restaurant was so ritzy they almost didn't let us in and so expensive we almost couldn't stay. But the food was delicious!

March 19, 1966

Wednesday was really a big day. We got up early and walked around the city of Honolulu a little. We made our way out to a gorgeous beach and waded in the surf. Of course we had to do a little shopping even though prices here are about what they are on the continent.

March 21, 1966

(As you see, I'm having difficulty finding time to finish this letter!) Our flight left Honolulu at 1:30 p.m. and was slightly rough due to the brisk headwinds. We crossed the International Date Line into Thursday and stopped at Wake

Island for refueling. We were there only about a half hour, but that was enough. The place is nothing but a dot of land in the midst of a huge ocean and it is really a forsaken place. Forsaken, that is, by everything but the U.S. military!

We flew from Wake Island to Tokyo but had only about an hour stop-over there, so we didn't even get out of the airport. It was getting dusk as we landed in Tokyo and the views of conical Mt. Fuji in the sunset were breathtaking. Due to those recent plane crashes in the area, I must admit I was on pins and needles both going in and coming out of Tokyo. A good many silent prayers were said but we had no trouble at all.

I was so tired by the time we left Tokyo that I refused the meal that was served en route, curled up in the corner and slept all the way to Hong Kong. The others reported that it was a very rough flight. I'm glad I slept!

We arrived in Hong Kong about 9:30 p.m. We were met there by the Mennonite representative who welcomed us and got us off to our hotel. The hotel was quite nice, even luxurious. We received a twenty percent discount as we are "missionaries," so it cost us $33.50 (U.S. dollars) for three nights, two breakfasts and one dinner for two of us. As you can see, prices are much less expensive in Hong Kong!

Friday morning we went on a tour which was sponsored by the Hong Kong Christian Welfare and Relief agency. We visited around the city at various projects sponsored by this agency such as refugee resettlement housing, a noodle-making factory, soup kitchens, technical training schools, roof-top schools, and community clinics. I was quite impressed by the quantity and diversity of the social welfare work being carried on in Hong Kong by religious organizations. It would certainly put the church in many parts of the U.S. to shame.

We spent Friday afternoon at the Hong Kong Church World Service office and then did a little shopping. Most of our shopping was just looking, however, because even though prices are great, I couldn't find what I wanted. Friday evening we had dinner with the Hong Kong director of CWS, Colin Morrison, and his wife. They are from Australia and formerly served in Korea. It was a lovely evening. But it got quite late and we were very tired.

Saturday morning and most of the afternoon, a Mennonite Pax man in Hong Kong, Bruce Harvey, took us around the city. We took the ferry across Hong Kong harbor from Kowloon to the Hong Kong side and drove around over there quite a bit. The Kowloon (mainland) side is quite level but the Hong Kong side is very mountainous. We wound round and round up the mountain to the tram car railway and proceeded to have a flat tire! Luckily we had a spare so we were soon on our way back down to the Kowloon side to do a little more shopping before we went home for an hour to rest.

The Mennonite director in Hong Kong, Mr. Friesen, invited us out for dinner (with chopsticks) at a Chinese restaurant and then to his home for dessert. We had a wonderful visit with them, but again it was late.

Sunday morning we were invited to a Chinese breakfast by a friend of one of my traveling companions. We overslept and almost missed it, but it was wonderful! The lady is a doctor at Hong Kong General Hospital and quite well to do. She was more than kind to us.

Our flight to Saigon left at 10:30 a.m. and it was a very pleasant trip. The plane was full of an assortment of Americans: a few military types, many U.S. Agency for International Development personnel, a few persons with Project Concern, some private businessmen and us!

More from Saigon.

March 23, 1966
Saigon, Vietnam

Dear Friends,

Saigon is a fascinating city. It is beautiful, bustling, quaint, harsh, Oriental. Everywhere, since my arrival, I am struck by the contrasts that make up life here. A woman walks down the road carrying her vegetables home from market as a military convoy thunders by; a girl in the graceful, flowing native dress (the *ao dai*) cycles past a woman on the street in stretch pants or other Western dress; large elegant French-style villas, and beggars in the street; a peaceful but noisy army of bicycles, scooters, and taxis streaming past a building fortified with barbed wire, sandbags, and armed guards; and, finally, the house in which we are currently living (one of the Mennonite residences in the city), whose name (*Em Dem*) translates to "Peaceful Villa." It is directly below one of the more heavily traveled flight paths out of the military airport a mile or two behind our quiet garden.

But everywhere, daily life goes on despite interruptions. Women go to market to do their daily shopping despite horrendous traffic conditions resulting from a vastly increased number of vehicles. Children go to school and play while planes thunder overhead. Women continue at their daily work in their homes wearing black mourning tags for husband or sons killed in the war. And one hears chatter and laughter on the street at night over the distant thunder of gunfire.

Some things have changed, however, with this American military semi-occupation. Rock and roll music blares from most radios; the row of bars across from the military airport does a box-office business; the airport has expanded to twice its original size; and prostitution is on the increase. These tangible changes wrought by the influx of Americans are obvious.

Underlying attitudes about the American "invasion" are harder to discern. Experienced Western travelers to Asia have commented that much feeling is often hidden behind the Oriental smile. I am only beginning to realize that truth. I can't help but wonder, every time we are stared at on the street, or followed by a group of children shouting, "O.K. Number One," (Anglo-Vietnamese slang for "very good"), how they really feel? Every time a shopkeeper serves me before one of his fellow countrymen who has waited longer, or when a taxi driver refuses to stop his empty cab for us, shaking his head emphatically "no," I wonder: what are they thinking?

Already in four days I've heard many varied opinions from Vietnamese on the status of their land. My only conclusion at this point is that people here, like those at home and elsewhere, are first and foremost individuals, possessing all the differences, variances, and peculiarities that the word implies. Generalities do not apply. These people are not a special kind of creature different from those I had known back home. They are simply people with a national problem.

This basic similarity stands, but, let me tell you, at times it seems like the only thing that's the same between U.S. life and Vietnamese life. A traffic jam of bicycles and horse carts; women doing construction work; servants doing the housework; inch and a half long cockroaches in the bathroom; and a siesta of an hour and a half every day are only the beginning of the differences. A little more difficult to adjust to is the need to bargain for everything I want to purchase, and a language composed of vowel and consonant syllable combinations in five tones. At this point the language is a complete riddle to me. But you all know how lost I am without the use of my tongue, so I expect to be able to learn a little!

Other adjustments include carrying water. Of the four days we've been here, we've had sufficient water pressure to fill the shower pipes only one of those days. You'd be surprised how genuinely thankful you can be for the simple things of life, like a lukewarm dip-and-pour shower once a day.

And electrical power failures! We've had power only two and a half of the last four days. There is not enough electrical power available to supply the entire city, so certain sections are cut off from electricity at regular times. The power failure which interrupted my letter last night was unexpected and included even the street lights, but electricity returned about midnight. The cut-off may have been intentional. In the ensuing darkness and quiet, as civilian traffic almost ceased, a greatly increased amount of military activity could be sensed around us, both close and far away. The dull thuds of bombs exploding a few miles away were louder and more frequent than usual. Several series of tracer bullets could be seen, although fairly far away.

It was reported to us that there was a small gathering of armed men near the post office downtown (needless to say, I didn't go out). The men here on the project reported that for a short time our front fence and gate were flanked by armed

guards as our whole street was apparently being closely
scrutinized. I was a little tense. I didn't sleep too soundly until
the electricity returned and I again heard the movement of
civilian traffic on the street.

   This is all just an attempt to state that last adjustment
which I am finding hardest to make—my proximity to war,
hate, destruction, death. I personally am not, and will not be,
in much more danger than if I were at home, I think. At times
during the day it's almost possible to forget that there is such
a thing as war in this lovely land. But at night, I am reminded
by bomb-thuds and flares. Last night I felt a twinge of the fear
familiar to those who experience war up close. It's not pleasant and my reaction was to be thankful for those armed
guards. I, too, am human. So my final and most difficult
adjustment will be to control and utilize this fear construc-
tively. My faith in God and in the power of love is being tried,
but I think it will survive!

3

In Study and Preparation

Newsweek
April 18, 1966

Turmoil In Vietnam: War Within A War?

Over the past twelve months, the U.S. has paid a steep price for its decision to deny the Communists possession of South Vietnam. The war now claims the lives of some 100 American soldiers each week, costs the American taxpayer $33 million a day and has so strained the resources of the armed forces that the Pentagon last week was forced to begin withdrawing 15,000 specialized troops from West Germany to flesh out training cadres in the U.S. Beyond all this, of course, is the intangible cost of the bitter divisions the war has created within the U.S. body politic. Last week, just as it was finally beginning to appear that these sacrifices would ultimately be rewarded with military success, South Vietnam once again erupted politically—and this time the eruption carried ominous overtones of anti-Americanism.

In Washington, some of the men most intimately involved in the conduct of the war expressed a feeling of bone-weary depression. Said one highly placed official: "I don't see how we can justify our casualties in Vietnam when the South Vietnamese appear to be more interested in squabbling among themselves than in fighting the common enemy.". . . .

The growth of anti-U.S. feeling in South Vietnam, of course, raises the danger that any future Vietnamese government—and perhaps even the Ky government if it survives—may be forced to flex its muscles against the U.S. in order to retain popular support. And if that muscle-flexing grows serious enough, it could become very difficult to explain continued U.S. involvement in South Vietnam to the U.S. public—and to the world at large. . . .

A Question Of Survival

The Vietnamese called it their "Week of Anger." Day after riotous day, growing numbers of demonstrators—students, Buddhists and members of the armed forces—rampaged through the streets of the country's major cities demanding the ouster of Premier Nguyen Cao Ky's military government. In the ancient imperial capital of Hué, 400 miles northeast of Saigon, 1,000 national policemen and some 3,000 soldiers of South Vietnam's crack First Division, led by their own officers, defiantly paraded with anti-government banners. Further south, in the resort city of Dalat, 3,000 rampaging students set fire to the top floor of a hotel housing the government radio station. In Saigon itself, riot police, after days of restraint, waded into a mob of 300 school boys who were attempting to stage a sitdown demonstration, and routed them with tear gas. And in the openly rebellious city of Da Nang, thousands of dissident troops barricaded themselves behind machine-gun nests and faced down a regiment of 1,500 loyal Vietnamese marines dressed in full battle gear.

While an incredulous Washington looked on with mounting concern, the protests suddenly turned blatantly anti-American. Students unfurled banners proclaiming "Down with U.S. Obstruction" and "Stop Interfering With the Vietnamese People's Just Aspirations." During one frenzied demonstration, a Buddhist leader led a crowd in a chant. "Nguyen Cao Ky!" he intoned through his bullhorn. "Da dao!" (Down with him!) answered the mob. "American imperialism!" he shouted. To which came the quick reply: "Da dao." As the protests gained momentum, the teen-agers began to roam the streets in search of Americans on whom they could vent their spleen. At one point, they attacked an American civilian engineer and his Vietnamese girl friend who were riding through downtown Saigon and burned their motorcycle. The next day they manhandled more than a dozen Americans, civilians and GIs alike, in a night-long orgy of rioting and destruction. . . .

All in all, it seemed last week that South Vietnam, a country already under deadly assault by a Communist enemy from without, had turned upon itself—and its staunchest ally—in a furious rage of self-destruction. . . .

April 3, 1966
Saigon

Dear Sisters and Families,

This has seemed like a rather long week for several reasons. For the first three days of the week, I was plagued by the commonest complaint suffered by traveling Americans: diarrhea, alias the "tropical trots" or the "Hanoi hops"! Tuesday it was so bad I lost seven pounds and stayed in bed most of the day, making quarter-hourly trips to the bathroom. Twenty-four hours and six diarrhea tablets later, I felt so much better that I went out for a coke. It was served on "unboiled water" ice and I got the trots all over again, but not quite as badly! That convinces me that I must go out frequently to eat or drink a little something so I build up my resistance! I feel fine now so it must be working.

We never have to worry about the food here at the house as the cook does a beautiful job. She is very careful in cleaning and cooking the food and serves delicious meals, both American and Vietnamese, the latter eaten with chopsticks, of course. We have Vietnamese food about three or four times a week. It usually consists of rice with meat or fish and vegetable gravies, and nuoc mam (the national dish, I guess) which is a fish sauce that tastes delicious but, I am told, smells terrible. Our Vietnamese meals also include much fruit, tea, and often a soup called pho (pronounced fuh) made with bean sprouts, parsley, noodles, and meat chunks in broth. The food is really delicious and seems lighter and easier to digest than Chinese food.

Besides the cook, for this household of nine or ten, we have three other female servants who do all the housework such as washing dishes, cleaning, laundry, marketing, ironing, setting table and, occasionally, minding the baby. This probably sounds extravagant to you, but remember that we have few "modern conveniences" and it would be virtually impossible for any woman to run a household alone here where marketing itself takes half of every day.

We also have a gardener who keeps the place in order, mans the big iron gate in front and serves as a kind of watchman. We have a driver for the car, too, who works only part-time. One brief look at Saigon traffic and you would under-stand instantly why a driver is necessary! All the servants except the cook and driver live in.

The house where we are living is a rambling, moderately well-to-do remnant of the French era. There are five rooms in the house (all with very high ceilings), a screened-in dining area, the servant's rooms, the kitchen and a low, flat building with 6 sleeping and 2 study rooms out back near a small garden. The grounds are surrounded by a high wall, topped in several places by jagged glass (remember, the French had their troubles here, too!) and entered only through an ornate, iron-grill gate out front. Our street, Duong Le Quang Dinh, is a poorly-repaired, dusty secondary street, wide enough for only one-way traffic when one of the frequent army convoys thunders by.

We are in Gia Dinh, a suburb of Saigon, and are not very near any large American establishments, military or civilian. It's really very nice out here as opposed to downtown Saigon; so much quieter and cleaner. We have trees and grass, less traffic and fewer Americans with money to throw around. The VNCS office, however, is right down in the heart of the city on Cong Ly street, across from the central market of Saigon.

We spent four hours and most of our April allowances at that market yesterday. It seems as if one can buy anthing from silk to sardines there. I got material for two dresses, one a silk Vietnamese *ao dai*, and a hat for $8.50. Not bad, huh?

A funny thing happened at the dressmaker's, though. One of my language teachers took me and my silk material to her dressmaker to get my *ao dai* made. It is a very close-fitting dress, so there was much measuring that needed to be done. As the seamstress measured me with her tape measure, she called out numbers to her daughter in the back room to record. The daughter began to giggle, louder with each number. After we left the shop, I asked my teacher what she was laughing at. She replied, with typical Oriental courtesy, "She never before see a so-big woman!"

I hope some of the pictures coming home are good. They are not being taken from the best view or angle but I do not want to offend people by taking pictures of them without asking permission. Language study continues full speed ahead but progress seems so slow. Next Saturday, two of us are invited out for lunch by a Vietnamese friend whose parents do not speak any English, so I'd better learn something quickly this week!

The English-speaking International Protestant Church here in the city is where I have attended the past two Sundays. It has a choir and needs sopranos so I may soon get back in the groove again. Their abundance of men and scarcity of women is a subtle evidence of the presence of the war.

We visited a less subtle indication this afternoon: the Victoria Hotel officers' billet which was bombed last Wednesday morning by V.C. terrorists. Six were killed, seventy-two wounded, the first two floors were destroyed, all windows of the other eight floors shattered and there was wide spread damage to buildings across the street. I was sickened by the sight and I wanted to cry as I remembered the morning's scripture, "He was wounded for our transgressions." Sights like that this Holy Week make it easy for me to think mankind hasn't improved much in 2000 years. Fine, strong, young men of several countries are still being killed for the sins of others; not on crosses but by submachine guns and plastic bombs. Yet a mass military pull-out seems impossible as political unrest increases. Is there an answer?

April 5, 1966
Saigon

Dear Folks,

Just a note of reassurance because I have no idea what the American press is reporting just now. I understand that *TIME* and *NEWSWEEK* are saying that internal unrest in this country is subsiding. That is not reporting of the news but hopeful prediction. Political unrest is widespread and the two most politically influential groups, the students and the Buddhists, have taken to street demonstrations again in cities all over the country.

Danang, in fact, is now in the control of a rebel government not sympathetic to the Saigon government. Its relationship to Hanoi is not clear yet. Hue, too, is in turmoil and even here in Saigon the street demonstrations have necessitated a six p.m. to six a.m. curfew for a few nights.

We do not know how long this will last but I cannot be too optimistic because of the variety and validity of the complaints. For example, Ky promised a constitutional government but little has been done about it yet. Much of the unrest is caused by anti-Western feelings and, of course, there may be some Communist assistance in these protests. However, from all that I can learn from first hand contacts, the most common and general feeling among all the Vietnamese people is that they are tired of war and all they want is peace and quiet. Of course most of the Western influence here is to perpetuate the war, so anti-Western feelings are logical.

As to our personal safety, we are a nonpolitical group and officially political neutrals. We try to keep ourselves distinct from American groups which are of a political or military nature. But we are Westerners, so we do have a plan for evacuation of all nonessential personnel from the country if and when it is necessary. And, believe me, nobody is more nonessential than those of us in language study! So relax!

We don't choose to be martyrs without a reason. At this point there would be no purpose served for those of us not yet on a project to stay here, should the situation become dangerous. That is my personal feeling (perhaps my yellow streak is showing through, too!) so I will not hesitate to leave if the need arrives. If, however, I were out on a work project and had served long enough to have established some respect and good relationships with those I was serving, then my decision would be very difficult, for there would be a reason to stay.

At any rate, this eventuality has not come up yet and in the meantime all I can do is study hard, be careful and obey curfew, present an honest picture of myself and my motives and pray! I'm trying to do all four! Of course, I'm a little frightened; but even more than that I'm sickened by the situation of this country and people which are being prostituted. I'm confused by the conditions and attitudes which cause or allow it and only part of them are imported!

P.S. Things look a little quieter today and curfew is nine p.m. to five a.m. tonight. That's a little progress but an evening with an early curfew really gets long! I'm glad for my ukelele!

April 11, 1966
Saigon

Dear Folks,

In reply to your letter of April first: I am present, partially accounted for, and realize that I am one day late with this letter. This delay is only partly accounted for by our busy social schedule but is primarily due to my extreme difficulty in finding a suitable secretary. I have at long last secured one. The U.S. government was kind enough to evacuate Hue and bring us another BVSer, Chris Kimmel, who has been serving there. As you can see, he is a "louzy writter." (That last sentence was an unauthorized addition by the secretary himself!)

Seriously, there are two reasons that I did not write this yesterday. Number 1, I finished a dress instead. I had bought the material in Hong Kong and our "housemother" Doris Longacre (who is the same age as I am) had a pattern for a loose shift. So I now have a new dress for church and other such occasions.

Number 2, I was in such a *terrible* depression it would not have been fair to you if I had written from the bottom of it! It is part of my own peculiar form of culture shock or homesickness, I guess. Yesterday, for the first time since my arrival, I would have accepted the gift of a ticket home: in fact, I would practically have sold myself into indentured slavery for it!

There are many reasons for this depression: fatigue, Easter Sunday, political unrest in the city, and a conversation with a USAID man. He was on our flight from Hong Kong to Saigon. We talked a little at that time (or I should say he talked, I listened) and lo, and behold, he turned up at our door Saturday. That was surprising since I had not told him my name, let alone my address. He says he is intrigued by my $10 a month salary and wants to know more about the program and purposes. I question that, as he is a fortyish "widower"; and if he had really wanted to know about the program, he would have listened to me describe it. At any rate, he made me confused and angry!

Earlier the same day another volunteer and I went out to lunch with a Vietnamese friend of hers. We had a lovely lunch with her family at their home. Her sister-in-law and stepfather do not speak English so it was also an opportunity to practice our scanty Vietnamese. This was the first time the other volunteer and I had been outside the front gate for six days. We had had a nine p.m. to five a.m. curfew for everybody every night last week and we Americans also had instructions from officials to "stay off the streets at all other times except on official business." So we respected this and stayed home.

However, we had made the luncheon plans before these "stay off the streets" precautions and we thought that we would be safe since it was in the middle of the day. Two of the fellows from here took us over on scooters and I sensed a change in attitude on the streets since I had been out last.

In addition to other effects, the six nights of demonstrations last week had resulted in two Americans being beaten, at least one a civilian. An American jeep and the civilian's Honda were burned by the demonstrators who were mostly students and Buddhists, protesting acts of Premier Ky's government and the American influence in it.

On our way out to catch a taxi home, I realized that we were the targets of various small objects such as stones and bottle caps which were being thrown. None of them had hit us yet. Our friend quietly said, "Continue on," and stepped behind us. The target practice stopped. I think it was mainly children who were throwing, but they learn attitudes from their elders.

Since Palm Sunday and the first of the current series of demonstrations here in Saigon, the disturbances have spread upcountry to all the major cities such as Hue and Danang, and most of the large towns such as Dalat and Nha-Trang. I have a persistent "beginning-of-the-end" feeling about the whole American effort here. I even question whether some of us, now in language study, will get out to our work projects upcountry before all American civilians are evacuated out of the country and the military will follow soon after. Such an exodus would leave behind a proud, torn little country which would rather make its own mistakes than be caught in the conflict of major powers and, because of sheer numbers, be dominated by one of them.

In other words, I almost expect that we will be asked to leave and perhaps before too long. This is not—repeat not—for general publication because it is just my own uninformed opinion. For our sakes, I hope I am wrong and that this is just the usual amount of unrest preceding a coup or something of that kind. I have not before, however, been aware of such a large element of anti-American feelings in the Vietnamese people as there is now. It is veiled most of the time by their Oriental courtesy, and in some people by an eagerness for the American dollar, but it is seething below the surface and, I think, runs deep. Do not think that this attitude of "beginning-of-the-end" is solely a result of my depression yesterday. It is a fact that I have been realizing for over a week and it greatly contributes to, rather than results from, the depressive state.

I hope you can tell by the letter that I am feeling better and a little more objective today. I'm discovering daily that the adjustments required by this situation which are difficult for me to make are in areas different than I expected and anticipated when I sat at home preparing myself. The control of fear of physical danger, for example, is easier than I anticipated. That is mostly because there is not as much imminent danger as I anticipated.

The adjustment to new foods, living habits, and new people has not been too difficult because here at our residence it's really not that different from home. I do not (or at least seldom) get desperately lonely or homesick for friends and family back home because I have good company here. On the other hand, I do long for good old fashioned "bull sessions," a tall glass of cold, fresh milk, the security of knowing that at least my words have been understood, the freedom to come and go at will and readily available transportation. Above all, I long for the security of knowing—not what tomorrow holds, (that can take care of itself!)—but which is the right path for today.

Those little daily decisions seem to be so much more important here than ever before. The simple act of accepting the luncheon invitation of a Vietnamese friend, for example, exposes us both to the anti-American feelings of others. If I decide to go to choir practice, I will have to defy instructions to Americans to stay off the streets except for official business. If I make the effort to utilize my scanty Vietnamese on one of our neighbors, I run the risk of being seriously misunderstood, as much because of my brown hair and round eyes as because of my poor language skills. I am beginning to understand what earlier amazed me: that everyday life continues in the midst of strife. I think it is essential that it does, because the war, by making the future completely uncertain and even nonexistent for some, thus makes the present vitally important. Every familiar act assumes a new significance and imparts a fragment of security.

My depression has passed for now but I must admit that my natural unbounded optimism is daily being tempered. Most difficult of all, my sense of purpose and direction for being here and the "rightness" of my presence here varies and fluctuates because of what I see and experience around me. A side effect of some of my own struggles is my new respect and agony for the fighting men, both American and Vietnamese. The American soldier must face all the difficulties I have found, plus his acute physical danger; and all at a much younger age than I.

Well, Armed Forces radio is optimistic (they have to be!) and last night for the second night in a row there were no demonstrations. It is so hard, in a city with censored press and abundance of rumor, to know what the truth really is but perhaps things are looking up again. Right now it seems that the election of a constitutional government would solve the problems of internal unrest but that will take months, even if the dissenting factions will wait for it. If not, it will take years. Because, as they renew violent protest, conditions will be less stable than ever and elections cannot take place in violence.

I think that I am rambling on because it is siesta hour and I am tired. Do please save these letters for me as my diary is too small to write this much in and besides I haven't time to write it twice!

Don't worry about me despite what you read in the papers. That is reporting only of external conflicts and I, like this country, am much more in danger from internal conflicts than external ones. But even in the struggles, rest assured that there are both human and divine assistance available to me here, too!

April 15, 1966
Saigon

Dear Folks,

Just a note to say I'm OK because I know this letter will reach you. As the political unrest continues mail service becomes uncertain also. I hesitate to use the APO services, even though they are available to us, because it appears hypocritical even to our nonpacifist coworkers here. I must do some more thinking on this point for myself. But, anyway, I am fine.

I'm sure you read or heard about the V.C. terrorist mortaring of the airport. Well, I slept through it although the airport is only about five miles from our house! Except for yesterday, curfew is back to normal twelve midnight to four a.m., and I think we are off "yellow alert." Yellow alert means to stay off the streets except for official business and then to proceed with caution. Political unrest continues. There was a demonstration yesterday, but more quiet, I think, since the constitutional assembly has been called into session.

Something is wrong with the flash on my camera. I hope it is just the batteries. It's hard or impossible to take the pictures I want to take here without offending people and getting dirty looks or worse. I can't afford hard feelings at a time like this when anti-American attitudes are already a dime a dozen! So, in the interest of international relations (and occasionally the safety of my own neck), I'm forgoing some pictures I would like to have.

Must go to siesta or I'll never last through the afternoon of language drills!

Love,

April 24, 1966
Saigon

Dear Folks,

This will be short for several reasons. It's late and I'm tired. Last night it was late, too, because a couple of us went to a concert at the Vietnamese-American Association. We enjoyed Vietnamese music, both instrumental and vocal, and also folk dances. The concert was great but not only did I get to bed late, I spent an hour of the short night in the bathroom with the "Hanoi hops" or diarrhea! What fun!

A friend from my BVS unit, Bruce Holderread, arrived in Saigon last week and has been out to the house for dinner. The two fellows who traveled here with me went to Pleiku this weekend to look over the project there as their prospective assignment. With the exception that the Pleiku airport was mortared nine hours before their arrival and a small battle was fought a little way out of town their second night there, it was an uneventful trip. I guess I'm becoming calloused or something but we just don't worry about each other or ourselves anymore. We pray and proceed! Another volunteer and I will go to visit the project at Nha Trang over the weekend of May 5 since there is a very good chance I will be assigned there and she will stay on in Saigon.

The only newsworthy political event of the week was the necessarily abrupt departure of A. J. Muste's group from the Committee for Nonviolent Action. The purpose of their Saigon trip was unclear to me but their cause was unpopular with a large group of Vietnamese students. They thought the group was here to advocate an "American pull-out" of Vietnam. Perhaps they were; it was never clear to me.

At any rate, the group scheduled a press conference last week which resulted instead in a small egg and tomato throwing riot. Consequently, the Vietnamese government refused to extend their visit visas and they were forced to leave. I get a little confused at the reactions of the Vietnamese people. They demonstrate in the streets against Americans who are engaged in a program of "violent assistance" but throw eggs at Americans advocating nonviolence! Well, so much for the Saigon scene—I'll write more when I'm more inspired.

Newsweek
May 2, 1966

The Campaigners

For more than a decade, Americans in ever-increasing numbers have arrived in South Vietnam loaded with advice on everything from how to raise pigs to the best tactics for killing Viet Cong. Last week, a group of U.S. citizens turned up in Saigon prepared to advise the Vietnamese people on how to turn the other cheek—and were promptly given the opportunity to practice what they preached.

Flying into the South Vietnamese capital with ordinary tourist permits, the six Americans—all pacifists sponsored by the New York Committee for Non-Violent Action—proceeded to hold a press conference in Saigon's City Hall. Led by the Rev. A. J. Muste, an 81-year-old veteran of pacifist causes, the group unfurled an array of antiwar posters and declared that South Vietnam should enter into negotiations with the Communist regime in Hanoi.

At that, angry Catholic students and youthful government agitators began pelting the pacifists with raw eggs, tomatoes and flash bulbs. Rushing up to the podium, student leaders broke into a chant: "Go home. Go home to North Vietnam." And next day, when the pacifists attempted to march to the U.S. Embassy, police hustled them off to the airport where they were put on a plane headed for Hong Kong.

April 30, 1966
Saigon

Dear Friends,

As you can well imagine, in this interval since my last letter to all of you, Saigon has become home to me. As I sit here in my *quan* (loose satin trousers worn by Vietnamese ladies to work in and by me to keep mosquitoes off my bite-scarred legs), I no longer notice the deafening thunder of a tank con-

voy rolling past the house and the sing-song chatter of the servants. The beggars on downtown streets get scarcely a
glance from hardhearted me and it's no longer an exciting
adventure to bargain for a cyclo (bicycle taxi) ride and go
downtown alone. The sights, sounds, and smells of Saigon
are no longer so different and exciting to me. Consequently I
now find myself collecting impressions of other and more
basic differences between my American cultural experience
and the Vietnamese culture in which I now find myself.

Just recently I've been increasingly impressed by
various attitudes of these people, such as their unbelievable
patience and stoicism. One often sees them standing in line
for hours with barely a change in facial expression and complaining, even about pain or a miserable existence, is
unbelievably rare.

Personal emotional reserve is obvious in almost every
contact with the Vietnamese. But they are capable of great
depth of emotional expression in a riot. There is an elaborate
system of social courtesies which governs all relationships;
yet they seem to lack concern for anyone outside their
immediate circle, family, or tribe. This indicates a duplicity of
feeling that is hard for me to understand. As one of my Vietnamese language instructors said yesterday, "Vietnamese
say one thing with mouth; think another thing in heart." But to
them this is not dishonesty. Nor is it dishonesty for a shop-
keeper to "take" a buyer for all he will pay.

Bribery, pocket-picking and theft of all sorts seem to be
amazingly common to this Westerner, used to strict law
enforcement. Americans, with their abundance of money,
are considered fair game. The Vietnamese are fiercely loyal to
their families, or, in the mountains, to their tribe, but they
seem to find it impossible to consider the needs or wishes of
those outside their circle. I've heard that even having concern
for patients is something that must be taught a Vietnamese
nurse; she does not develop it naturally. On the other hand,
the Vietnamese are beautiful, creative in arts and have
incredibly strong family ties.

Political affairs, also, are affected by lack of concern for
those outside the family and inability to plan for the future.

(Theirs hasn't been secure enough to plan for in twenty-five years so why bother to try?) The brand of "nationalism" that I'm used to in a democracy, (pride in, loyalty to, and responsibility for a national government) is largely lacking here from what I can see. This, too, no doubt, is a result of the past twenty-five years of war. In more recent years it seems they have seldom had anything to be proud of or loyal to in the way of national government.

I think it's partly due to national temperament also. The populace, especially Buddhists and students, are masters at disruption and protest. I question how much loyalty an elected government would generate, especially if it were designed along the lines of a democracy. Although the people say an elected government is what they want, it requires an educated and concerned public. I question whether American democratic ideals are workable in the Orient ever, but especially not here and now. If fair elections really could be held throughout the south part of this country right now, the majority elected government would, I think, be Communist-leaning. My opinion!

The political unrest and riots of the past month have really forced all of us to think along these lines. If you have been reading the newspapers about Vietnam you will know what I mean. Let me hasten to assure you that the only inconvenience the rioting caused us was the necessity of staying off the street except for official business. Not having any official business, that meant that I didn't leave the house for six days straight. Except for this and having as extra house guests those who had been evacuated from other areas due to rioting, it was business as usual.

I, too, have had to read the news magazines to find out exactly what was happening. From the publicity here about the riots two weeks ago, it seems that there are about three major themes in the protests: first, "corruption in the present Saigon government: they have betrayed the true revolution." Certain acts of the present government, such as summary dismissal of General Thi, discrepancies in administration of various agencies and distribution of government relief commodities, use of troops in Danang and censorship of the press, among other things have undermined the confidence the populace has in its government.

Second, "Free elections and constitutional government without American interference." The desire for an elected constitutional government is a major rallying point for the protesters.

Third, "Vietnam for the Vietnamese: Americans, get out of politics." There are also protests against American intervention in the government, that is, against the U.S. backing of Premier Ky in some projects which seem questionable to some of the Vietnamese, such as use of U.S. military planes to transport Vietnamese troops to Danang to fight their countrymen.

These are reasonable enough requests, it seems to me, but the rioting got somewhat out of hand the latter part of the week of April 7 and 8. Two Americans, at least one a civilian, were beaten, and their vehicles burned. Rioting had begun in Hue and Danang the week previously and Americans had been evacuated from those areas to Saigon. As the atmosphere got more tense here we got out our own evacuation plan and got it in order, just in case. Then, through a series of Buddhist-government negotiations, concessions were made by the government and the demonstrations ended.

Upon the Buddhist threat of resumed demonstrations, the government convened the constitutional assembly on April 13 and Saigon has been politically quiet since. The northern provinces of Hue and Danang, after a period of quiet, are becoming uneasy again. Fairly responsible sources of information here predict a Catholic demonstration tomorrow and one by Buddhists on Monday. Here we go again! There is so much more protest from all groups than constructive action in regards to the internal politics of the Republic of Vietnam. I find myself really wondering much of the time what the American military is doing here defending a government whose very constituency has taken to the streets to protest it!

That's only politics—there's a war going on here, too, you will remember. We are reminded frequently by newspapers, military convoys, and letters from home. The military action of the war is far from Saigon: at least three miles! But even here, the terrorist activities keep us from forgetting. Two days ago a satchel bomb killed ten and wounded thirty, all civilians, and the airport was mortared a week ago and quite a bit of damage was done.

Last week an attempt was even made on the police station a few blocks down the street from us. It was unsuccessful but the grenades (used as a diversionary tactic) and the misplaced explosive charge did injure several people. Incidentally, here at the house it was a good rehearsal for the "real thing" if it should ever come.

To us here in the house it sounded like the small arms fire and grenades were in our own back yard. It was a fantastic study in reaction. We all stopped what we were doing and looked at one another. Nobody panicked even though we were all a little frightened. As the action continued, the women calmly and quickly gathered up their little children; the men shut the doors, curtained the windows and turned out the lights. We all moved to the center of the house and sat down on the floor away from the windows.

We waited in the dark silence for several minutes, then began to resume our conversation and joking. We even dealt out another hand of cards, still on the floor. We were in no danger at all as the action was several blocks away, but I was glad for the experience. I would have really felt cheated if I had not had at least one "heroism in the face of danger" story to bring home!

Language study has occupied our entire time for the past two months and for me it has been fascinating. Vietnamese is a tonal language. The same syllable can have five different meanings depending upon which of five tones is used in speaking it. It gives the language a sing-song sound and is very complicated for a Westerner to learn. After two months of study, I think I am more confused about the language than I was before.

Not only is it a problem of learning pronunciation, tones, vocabulary and grammar, but one must learn new customs of speech. For example, one seldom comes right out and says what is really meant. Rather it must be hinted at. "Who speaks little Vietnamese better?" is the way the Vietnamese would say "Who speaks Vietnamese lousier?" The crowning blow is that this language doesn't seem to have a word for "no." One must say, "Yes, I cannot" or "Yes, I do not." That somehow seems symbolic! On the other hand, the grammar and pronunciation are fairly easy, so I'm thankful for that.

At any rate, my problems will soon be solved (or just begun) because language study for us is over Wednesday and we start on our permanent projects the first of the next week. The two young men I travelled with will be going to Kontum and Pleiku; my roommate will stay in Saigon and I go to NhaTrang.

The Mennonites help to staff a hospital-clinic at Nha-Trang, established some years ago by the Vietnamese Protestant Church. The clinic provides both in-patient and out-patient care. It is small and is staffed by one doctor and about three nurses, and they are short one nurse now. Because of political instability and military security changes, the proposed new projects upcountry are opening up very slowly. Danang is out for security reasons and Quang Ngai is the only new project opening just now. So I will go to Nha-Trang, a previously established project, but serving in an area of need.

I'm eagerly awaiting the trip for many reasons. I'll be glad to get back to work after this four month "vacation" from nursing. NhaTrang is reported to be one of the beauty spots of Vietnam and the hospital is right on the coast of the South China Sea with access to a beach. I know nothing about the project but I am eager to get started "earning my keep," and I will be writing you from there.

For many reasons I welcome this opportunity to get to work, but I think most important is a sense of accomplishment; of doing something. Language study doesn't provide this sense of achievement and it is, at times, very difficult for me not to fall prey to discouragement. As we were warned in BVS training, there are other problems, too, such as use of time, group living, communication breakdown. But for me, here and now, a tendency to become discouraged about my own contribution, even more about the entire Vietnam situation, is even more of a problem than fear which I am learning to control.

There seem to be no answers to the problems here and my contribution towards finding a solution is so small. The powers of the world seem intent on following a policy of "me-first-ism" and all of us here in Vietnam stand on the battlefield of a conflict of political generalities. Those involved seem to have forgotten that God created people and taught them to love each other long before they learned to practice politics!

But I'm here not as a politician or even as a news reporter. Only as a Christian nurse, and a dove! I am very grateful for the opportunity of living here with the Mennonite group, in daily contact with many people whose Christian commitment provides both concern and hope. So, while the situation is not always as pleasant and carefree as it might be, it's been several weeks since I've considered accepting a ticket home, even if one were offered free!

The mail service here is rather unreliable, both in and out. I say a little prayer for the safe arrival of every letter I send! So far, I have answered every personal letter I've received except from family. So, if you've not received an answer, try again. It's not that I didn't write. Your letters make me both happy and homesick, but both feelings are pleasant.

I remember you in my prayers and thank you for yours in my behalf. Please pray not for my safety but that I might have purpose, courage and the strength to love!

May 3, 1966
Saigon

Dear Mother,
(and anyone else to whom Mother's Day greetings apply),

Mother's Day falls somewhere within this month, I understand; so I shopped for greeting cards today. I know that there are some somewhere in this bustling city but I didn't have time to go to the right places. So I'm afraid you'll have to be content with just a plain letter. Happy Mother's Day, whenever it is!

My roommate and I are cutting language study this
morning to go to the American Embassy to get my passport
renewed. We also need to do a little shopping for a party we've
planned for our language instructors tomorrow night.
Tomorrow will be our last day of formal study with them. I am
leaving for NhaTrang some time on Thursday and won't be
back here for quite awhile. My roommate will be starting work
at the Seventh Day Adventist Hospital here in Saigon next
Monday. Our other two traveling companions will be going to
Pleiku next week.

I'm very much looking forward to going but I shall be sad
to leave all the friends I have made here in Saigon. But that's
the progression of life, is it not? I will be glad to get started to
work, and the hospital there sounds very interesting. If you
wonder why I'm not more newsy about my project assignment in this letter, it's because I explained in my April 30
newsletter. I sure hope it gets there!

In setting my affairs in order in preparation for going upcountry, getting my visa extended, passport renewed, money
for travel, travelers' checks in the safe, and so on, I suddenly
realized that I had not written a will while I was at home. Not
that I own anything of value to anyone else, but I do not want
you, the rest of the family, to face court costs to obtain what I
want you to have. Enclosed find a statement of my wishes in
this respect. In the absence of a lawyer, I have composed it
myself and, due to lack of a notary public, have had it signed
by two witnesses. Please put it on file with my insurance
policies and other important papers. I think it would be better
than nothing in event a will were needed. This is really a great
"will-writing" time here in Saigon. Things are as quiet as a
Sunday School picnic, and there's a special "off-season" rate
for those who "will in peace-time and avoid the rush!" So here
it is.

We're having a circus this week around the house. Our
houseparents, Paul and Doris Longacre, are gone on vacation and none of us left here speak Vietnamese nearly as well
as our housemother. The servants speak no English. For
some reason, they come to me with their questions and I am
most often delegated by the others here to give the servants

instructions about the household work. It's really a riot because they always say they understand me. But I'm never really sure of what I've said myself, so I can't imagine that they can actually understand me!

4

In Adjustment to Work

Newsweek
April 1, 1966

The Big E At Work

They call it Yankee Station—a rolling, quadrangular expanse of blue-green water that lies mostly north of the 17th parallel, where the South China Sea joins the Gulf of Tonkin. From Yankee Station, ships of the U.S. Seventh Fleet's Task Force 77 operate around the clock to launch bombing strikes against military targets in Communist North Vietnam. Over four months ago, Task Force 77 was joined by the 86,000-ton U.S.S. Enterprise—the world's first nuclear-powered aircraft carrier—and the Big E's arrival brought a new dimension to the war the Navy fights. Last week, *Newsweek* Saigon bureau chief William Tuohy flew out to join the Enterprise and cabled this report:

From his command post high on the navigating bridge, the Enterprise's skipper, an unflappable 44-year-old captain named James L. Holloway Jr., looks down on the carefully choreographed ballet of carrier warfare that unfolds on the flight deck far below. Every twenty seconds during the launching periods, as regularly as the tick of a metronome, one rocket-laden jet bomber after another is hurled off of the carrier's 4.47-acre deck with a whoosh of steam, the whiplash crack of catapult cables and the never-ending banshee howl from the bombers' tailpipes. . . .

One typical morning this week, the Big E's 140 pilots were up at 2:30 a.m., dressed in flight gear and off for a briefing on the day's strike from Lt. Comdr. Jude Lahr, 34, leader of Attack Squadron 93. The inevitable tension was there, but there were no dramatics. Just before Lahr began his briefing, another pilot returned from an earlier attack with his personal weather report. "There was goo [fog] all the way," he said, "right down to 900 feet."

Then Lahr began to brief his men, referring when necessary to a large battle map. "We will make one pass from this direction, and then we'll come in this way, drop our stuff and evade by doing this [here he makes some pilot's short-hand gestures over the map] . . . Watch your leader and watch your tail . . . If you have to bail out, head for the ocean. Try to slow down before you eject. If I go down [here he nods to his second-in-command] you have the flight . . . Any questions?" There are none, and Lahr says, "OK, let's go." . . .

Air boss Smith goes to work: "Heads up on deck," his steady voice crackles over the radio system. "It's time for complete flight-deck uniform—helmets on, goggles down . . . Now stand clear of the props. Stand clear of jet intakes and exhausts . . . Start the helo. Now start the Spad [Navy lingo for a prop plane] . . . Start the go jets . . . Launch the helo . . . Five minutes to launch . . . Thirty seconds to launch. Now launch aircraft."

With an ear-splitting screech, the aircraft on the four catapult bridles are slingshotted off the ship into the air. "Let's get 103 on the starboard cat," says Smith. "103 just went down, boss," the word comes back. "All right," says Smith, "get it the hell out of the way and give me another go bird." Within seconds, the flight-deck crew substitutes another jet . . .

"Launch completed," Smith announces over the bull-horn. Then, as an earlier strike force prepares to return to the carrier, he gives out the orders again. "Heads up on deck. We've got a recovery flight coming in five minutes, and I want that angle deck cleared." . . . .

In the dark, landings are even trickier. Over the radio, the air controller says: "307, you are 10 miles out and on course. Now do dirty [let flaps down]. Now turn left . . . Keep coming. Do you have the ball?" The pilot sees the orange light of the "meatball" in the illuminated lens on deck and guides his plane in for a perfect landing.

In 85 days of combat operation, the Enterprise has flown nearly 10,000 sorties—and lost only seventeen planes. As a result, morale among the pilots and crew stays consistently high, even though there is a chronic problem of fatigue. Says one medical officer: "A fellow who can catch a nap on a pile of bombs will last longer than the man who has to have his sleep regularly at night." And a weary pilot adds: "Happiness is four hours' sleep."

May 7, 1966
NhaTrang

Dear Family,

Greetings from Chan-Y-Vien Tin-Lanh (Evangelical Clinic). It is located just about a hundred yards from the South China Sea, just north of NhaTrang. This will be my home for the coming year and, judging from what I've seen since we arrived at 5:30 p.m. Thursday, I think I'll like it. The hospital is a part of a series of institutions (orphanage, hospital, and Bible school seminary) all owned and operated by the Vietnamese Protestant (Tin-Lanh) Church. The church is the result of the missionary efforts of the Christian and Missionary Alliance church in this country.

The hospital was started in the late 1950s by the Tin-Lanh church but there is a shortage of national medical personnel to staff the institution. So they made an agreement with the Mennonite Central Committee to provide almost all the professional staff. MCC is now co-operating with Vietnam Christian Service in relief and medical work in this country and they are sharing staff. So that is how I find myself on an MCC project. To save myself from having to write a lot of information twice, I'll get a newsletter out soon containing all the details and descriptions of my new home.

The flight up here on Thursday was a once-in-a-lifetime experience. At least I hope it was only once; I'm not sure I could take it again! First, there were two delays; one because the first plane had no brakes and the second because it took an hour to fix the radio on the second plane. We finally got airborne in less than perfect weather. Our craft was a tiny, two-engine, seven-seater Beechcraft. When we turned inland toward our first scheduled stop, we ran smack into an electrical storm which would have made a big plane shudder.

The pilot headed out to sea to get around the storm. We got out about fifteen miles and were flying low enough to see the foam on the white caps. And still we were being tossed by the storm like a model plane. To top it off, we couldn't make radio contact due to the surrounding electricity of the storm! It was terrible! I cannot ever remember feeling so completely scared. Fear welled up in me like a hot, throbbing fluid. But there was absolutely nothing that could be done but grip the seat arms tighter, wait, and pray. So that's what I did. Even with the fear pulsing in every joint, I couldn't bring myself to pray for safety but only for strength for all of us.

It must have been provided, because none of us panicked. After about thirty minutes, we landed safely at Nha-Trang airport. I nearly kissed the ground when I got out. That's what I call an A-1 lesson in the practical application of prayer.

Well, I'm running out of space and I want to send this back to Saigon with my friend so that she can mail it for me. The mail service is so much better there than up-country. Don't worry—I'm really not in any more danger than you are. Besides, I'm not planning on any more plane trips for awhile.

May 12, 1966
NhaTrang

Dear Sisters,

This is hardly the day to write a letter to you as I am scraping the bottom of "culture shock" or something. I am in a foul humor and have been for about two days. But I have today off so I'd better write while I have the time.

Mother has probably informed you that I am now upcountry and out on my permanent work project. I am at the Evangelical Clinic (Chan-Y-Vien Tin-Lanh). The clinic is very near the beach and a good swimming area. The scenery here is indescribably beautiful with mountains surrounding our little bay of the sea. The view from our front yard includes an island and fishing boats plying their trade. The only unpleasant part of the scenery is that there is a Vietnamese military academy just down the beach from us. So our peace and quiet is regularly punctuated by flares and blasts as the military students practice. But then, one can't have everything, can one? They tell me that there is a war going on here!

It is rather difficult for me to describe the hospital to you right now. I am finding every day and night of work a painfully frustrating experience. In spite of the two months of language study, my communication skills are woefully inadequate. I can see already that there will be many adjustments that I'm going to have to make to such things as lack of supplies and equipment, Oriental temperament, lack of staff, overwork, and other things, no doubt. At this point, I definitely feel like more of a liability than an asset. But, don't fret; I know that I will get over the shock of it all soon enough. Then I'll be able to settle down to the task of studying and learning some of the things about which I now feel so painfully stupid.

There is bed space for about thirty-five or forty patients but just now we have fifty patients, five of them lying on the floor in the hall and about seven on the floor of the front porch. The out-patient department sees about a hundred patients a day four days a week and the doctor does surgery twice a week, about three to six cases a day. Most of the surgery he does is eye surgery. Trachoma, cataract and entropion, all diseases of the eye, are so very much more common here than they are in the States.

As you can no doubt guess from this description, the schedule of work hours for everybody around here is unbelievable. Everybody is supposed to have one day a week off but during the other six days it's twenty-four hours duty for the doctor and one of the four of us nurses on alternate days. That's part of my trouble now: I'm just plain tired! I don't see how the folks here have done it for as long as they have. I'm sure I'll get used to it but it's a little rough right now!

When I regain my natural good humor and equilibrium, I'll write out a more detailed description of the whole project here, but I'm not quite able to give you a fair picture just now. Mom and Dad will soon be getting back the pictures that I took so generously during my first few days after I arrived. If you get a chance to see them, you will be able at least to get an idea of what the place looks like.

I guess by this time you are approaching the close of another school year. School closes here between April and the first of August, so just now the children are underfoot all day. I have been complaining about medical conditions here but conditions in education are not any better. Only a relatively small percentage of children can attend school due to the enormous number of children and the lack of facilities and teachers.

One of my Vietnamese language instructors was also a public school teacher. She said that the children, and a few lucky adults, go to school in three shifts every day. She had between eighty-four and ninety in her classes. Seeing the unbelievably large number of children and the real hunger for education among many of the Vietnamese people of all ages, I can believe it. Unfortunately, after the years of basic education, it appears that bribery and influence are more important in advancement in the school system than intelligence and hard work. But, then, in more areas than education, one must get used to the fact that money works miracles here.

Well, my dears, I could write a book but you are saved that torture by my lack of time. Besides, in the mood I am in today, it would never pass the censors in Saigon! I think of you all so very often and wonder how you are doing. It's not that I'm homesick, and I don't think I'd come home if I got the chance, but I sure do miss all of you!

May 18, 1966
NhaTrang

Dear Friends,

Since I wrote you last, I have terminated language study, not because I have learned everything, I assure you! Instead, I have moved to my permanent work project. Some of you knew, I think, that I was originally scheduled to go to Danang to work in refugee health services there. As you no doubt can tell by the newspapers, that is no place for Americans to be just now, so it has been impossible to open the proposed project there. In fact, political and military instability in the whole country has made it very difficult to open any of the proposed new projects. As I write this letter, Vietnam Christian Service has two fellows on an agricultural project in Hue, five people in Quang Ngai in community development and, here in NhaTrang, there are six of us in medical work.

Chan-Y-Vien Tin-Lanh, or Evangelical Clinic, is located just about four miles outside of NhaTrang. If you check the map, you will see that city is located directly on the coast of the South China Sea. The clinic is north of NhaTrang and just far enough out that it is considered "off limits" for the U.S. forces. Anything beyond three miles outside of town is officially considered "Viet Cong controlled territory." That makes it very nice for us. We are in no danger here, being a nonpolitical and non-American institution and we have peace and quiet, as well as our own "private" beach less than a hundred yards from the front door of the Clinic.

The Clinic is actually both hospital and clinic, and is one of several institutions located near each other here on the seashore. All of them are owned and operated by the Vietnamese Protestant Church, the Tin-Lanh Church. There is an orphanage, a Bible School Seminary and our hospital. Most of the staff of all three institutions are Vietnamese but, because Tin-Lanh Church is very short on medical professional staff, the Mennonite Central Committee has supplied additional professional staff for the hospital since 1958.

At the present time, there are three nurses (besides myself, that is, and after only a week of work I don't count for too much yet). There is also one medical doctor and one Pax man, the Mennonite term for a young man who is doing civilian service as an alternative to military service. Our Pax man serves as general handyman, mechanic, administrator of the hospital and occasionally surgical assistant. The Vietnamese staff of the hospital numbers about twenty.

I'm including a roughly sketched map of the hospital; remember I'm a nurse and not an architect or map-drawer! Our little institution provides three types of care: out-patient care (note the clinic and clinic porch "waiting room"), resident care for TB patients (see the TB houses), and in-patient care (provided in the main hospital in front of the clinic.) The out-patient clinic sees more than a hundred patients on four days of the week. Every patient is seen by a nurse; then those requiring medical attention see the doctor. Everything from the "fatigue of motherhood" to leprosy passes through that clinic; patients are given what care and medications we have available for them. Most of the work has to be done through interpreters which only adds to the general confusion.

If patients seen in the clinic are seriously ill or need surgical treatment, they are admitted to the hospital. Accommodations there are simple; a bed frame with wooden slats on which is placed a grass mat for the patient to lie on. If there are enough sheets, one may be provided to cover the mat. Family members who stay with the patients sleep on the floor in the hall or under the patient's bed.

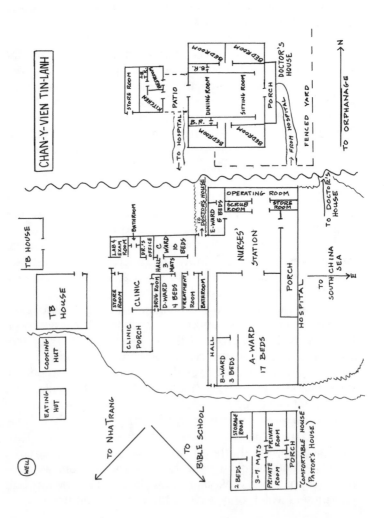

Behind the hospital are two small houses, the TB houses, which contain nothing but wooden platforms on which the TB patients stretch out their grass mats. The forty or fifty patients housed in these two buildings stay for periods varying from two months to two years. The clinic staff provides their medications which are distributed to them once a week. They are followed by periodic X-rays when indicated and the hospital staff makes occasional rounds on them. Otherwise, the residents of the TB houses take care of themselves.

That's not really as cruel as it sounds to those of you who are used to the conventional sparkling white, sterile U.S. hospital. Life, including hospital life, is a little simpler here than in the States. The essentials of life for the poor Vietnamese are only a grass mat and two bowls of rice a day. So, when they come or bring someone to the hospital, they must also bring cooking pots and a small store of rice. The rice will be needed during the trip to the clinic, for it may take several hours or days and there is not a restaurant available at every crossroad.

The rice will also be needed during their stay here at the hospital, because the hospital does not provide any food to the patients. The hospital charges only ten piasters (about ten cents) for a clinic fee and only about fifty piasters for an admission fee to the hospital. Even these modest fees sometimes cannot be paid. When that is the case, the patient is cared for anyway. On such a limited income, the hospital simply cannot afford to feed the resident patients, let alone the patients' families who come to the hospital with them. So the families, who stay with the patient to help us care for them, must provide all their own food while they are here.

The inpatient hospital is where I have been spending almost all of my time. The hospital has approximately thirty-six beds in its five wards and three rooms but at the present time we have a census of about fifty. We have three mats in the hall, about ten on the front porch, plus a few extras stuck in here and there in the main wards. As I mentioned before, members of the patients' families come to the hospital with them and stay, doing cooking, laundry, and the direct care of the patient until they are well enough to go home.

The hospital has two small houses out back in which the wives and mothers (or fathers and children) of the patients can fix their food, draw water, and do laundry. As short as we are of staff, we couldn't get along without the family members caring for their own. But, believe me, at times this place resembles a three-ring circus with two hundred people crowded on the outpatient department porch, forty TB patients, fifty inpatients, and at least that many healthy family members wandering around.

Besides learning to delegate nursing care to family members, there are a few other adjustments that I have to make. For example, starting an IV is difficult enough for me any time. I find it completely impossible to do while sitting on the floor trying to find a vein which hasn't collapsed yet in a patient who has had diarrhea for ten days. The patient's body is covered with tiny nicks, and perhaps a little mud or cow dung because the family took the patient to the local "Chinese doctor" first.

For me to scrub in surgery is a laugh at any time. As some of you know, I have always had six thumbs on each hand in the operating room. It is really hilarious, however, when my job is first (and only) assistant to the surgeon. In that role, one of my duties is to shoo the flies off the "sterile" field without touching them with my sterile gloves which would contaminate them (the gloves, not the flies!)

Patient-doctor and patient-nurse communication is always a problem. Add to that the fact that the patient speaks a different language than the doctor and nurse (and even a slightly different dialect than I studied in Saigon.) You come up with a real source of confusion and frustration for all of us. We do have some interpreters, but there are never enough to go around and they, too, need a day off occasionally.

This all sounds very humorous now, but I can assure you that there are times when it is not funny at all. For example, last week we had both a typhoid patient and a cholera patient on IV's and had only one bottle of any kind of IV fluid left. Last night we lost a twenty-seven year old woman with pneumonia and severe anemia because she needed blood or packed cells and, of course, we have nothing of the kind. We have no oxygen; we have to be very conservative with linen because we're fortunate to have enough sheets to go around one to a bed. The doctor does surgery two days a week with a minimum of equipment in a field in which he has had little special training, eye surgery. And, often after we've put in our fifty-five to sixty hour weeks, we, or at least I, (I can't speak for the others!) can get pretty grouchy. But still the patients keep coming!

For those of you who are medically oriented, perhaps you would be interested in what types of medical conditions we see most commonly here. It seems that one of the most predominant and dangerous problems is tuberculosis. Then there are all sorts of other problems we didn't study in nursing school because "they just don't occur anymore," such as: typhoid fever, cholera, malaria, occasionally leprosy (these patients we refer to the nearby leprosarium), a case or two of bubonic plague, malnutrition and very frequent occurrence of trachoma, cataract, glaucoma and entropion. Of course stroke, trauma and burns, heart disease (but no infarcts), ulcer and colitis, appendicitis and cancer are more universal and we see those here, too.

It's going to be a big job and quite a challenge in many ways, as I have illustrated above. Although we are not a politically oriented institution, just being in Vietnam is a political challenge for an American. Our answer to that challenge here at the clinic is to treat a person to the best of our ability according to his need, never inquiring into his political loyalties. To be practical about it, that philosophy is good protection to us here at the hospital. But that is only one of the side effects of treating people as persons and not political pegs. Pain, disease, and dying are far more important to people the world around than communism, capitalism or any other "ism," and that's the level of life we're dealing with here.

So in spite of all the difficulties of our lot as I have listed them above, don't feel sorry for me, because right now I wouldn't trade with any of you. It's a good thing you didn't ask me last week because I would almost have walked the whole way home. But that was just last week!

Besides a great bunch of people to work with, I have indescribably beautiful mountain and seaside scenery, and an almost private swimming beach right here within walking distance. Not too many of you have it that good! It is very peaceful and quiet here and, if it weren't for the Vietnamese military academy just down the beach with their teaching maneuvers, we could almost forget that a war is going on at all. The more the beauty of the place and the charm of the people grow on me, the sadder and sicker the whole war business makes me!

Thanks to all of you for your letters; they are a constant source of encouragement to me. I continue to try to keep them answered, but I understand that the mail service from NhaTrang is even more unreliable than from Saigon. My only feelings of homesickness continue to be when I read your letters and wish I could be with you. But, of course, in my thoughts and prayers, I often am.

P.S. Folks,

What an extra specially pleasant evening we had tonight. We had company up from Saigon and how these Mennonites can sing! We sang hymns for two hours while I pumped at a very old, rickety, little bellows organ. Then, when I got tired, we sang folk music for another hour. Everyone of the group here sings and the doctor even plays the guitar!

5

At Work

Newsweek
June 13, 1966

Fiery Rebellion

A 19-year-old nun named Vien Ngoc walked slowly out of the Saigon headquarters of the Buddhist Institute into the cool spring night. After unrolling a rice-straw mat on the pavement, she seated herself, folding her slender legs in the lotus position of her faith. She whispered a prayer. Calmly she then doused her clothing with gasoline and lit a match. In seconds the flames flared across her body and face, and as the girl toppled over backward in a charred heap, hundreds of Buddhists crowded close, kneeling, chanting and lighting long red candles near her feet. Finally, what was left of the nun was pushed into a crude litter made of blankets and carried inside the compound where Buddhist activists raised a banner over Vien Ngoc reading: "Sacrifice and sacrifice much more in order to warn the irresponsible and heartless people about the crimes of the Americans and the Thieu-Ky lackeys."

Despite the calls of moderate Buddhist leaders for an end to "self-destruction," the fiery suicide of Vien Ngoc was only one shocking note in a week of horror. "Sacrifice" was demanded by the militants, so a 30-year-old monk burned himself to death in the main pagoda in Dalat; a 17-year-old schoolgirl did the same in rebellious Hué—right in the middle of Ta Street. And in other parts of the country, Buddhists slashed their veins and chopped off their fingers in a grisly show to arouse rebellious emotions and bring down the military junta of Premier Nguyen Cao Ky.

May 30, 1966
NhaTrang

Dear Sisters,

For the life of me I can't remember whose turn it is to receive a letter from me this time. I'm off tomorrow so I can afford to stay up later than usual tonight to get caught up on letter writing. With the heat, a fifty to sixty hour work week and swimming in the turbulent surf in my free time, I find that by ten o'clock I'm exhausted! It hasn't been quite as hot this week as it was before because we had some off-season afternoon rains. Unfortunately, however, this tends to activate the mosquitoes who rest during the dry season. So this week we not only have the seasonal heat but also the unseasonable (and I could also say unreasonable!) mosquitoes. Another one of the nurses and I have decided to buy some mosquito netting by the yard on our next trip into town and I will whip us up a little mosquito deterrent out of it.

That reminds me. I haven't told you anything about the rest of the staff here, have I? Thumbnail sketches, then. My roommate, Marcy Weber, is a Canadian RN in her early twenties, and she has been here about ten months. She is in charge of the clinic staff and knows more about the hospital than any of the rest of us. Therefore, unofficially, she is more or less the director of the nursing staff.

Emma Lenzman, another Canadian nurse is about fifty years old. She has been here for about eight months and is in charge of the operating room and surgery. She helps out in the clinic on busy days and both of them fill in at the hospital, too. Mostly because of her age, she finds it a little harder to adjust to some of the inconveniences and inadequacies of our situation here. But she is blessed with a sense of humor that usually sees her through such situations.

Another nurse from Pennsylvania Mennonite country and Goshen College, Ruth Yoder, has been here for two months working temporarily before she returns to Saigon for more language study. She will then return here to develop the plans for a nurses' training program to be organized here at the clinic. She is in her thirties and spent some time working on a Mennonite mission and service project in Peru before coming to Vietnam.

Dr. Linford Gehman is in his early thirties and also from Pennsylvania. He went to medical school in Philadelphia, I think. He has been here for about a year and a half and, right now, is the only doctor here. Therefore, he is, unofficially at least, on call all the time. We hope this is a temporary situation. He is a folk-music fan and a better guitar player than administrator of either the hospital or the unit. He works very hard at practicing medicine and so has little time remaining to spend on the internal functionings of the hospital which, by default, are also his responsibility.

Carl Kauffman, our Pax man, is from Kansas and serves as our combination surgical assistant, hospital administrator, mechanic, maintenance man, accountant, supply advisor, and bookkeeper. He had spent ten months working on a project in Hong Kong before he was transferred here about a year ago. He is in his early twenties and speaks Cantonese (a Chinese dialect) better than Vietnamese. All of these folks are Mennonites but from various divisions and boards of the church.

For these last few weeks, the hospital has not been quite as busy as it was that first week I arrived. I'm not sure if we have less work now or if I'm just learning my way around a little better. My biggest source of frustration continues to be language inadequacy. I never realized before how essential shared communication is in so many widely varied areas of living and relating to people. I know it would help if I could discipline myself to a program of daily study but so far, in what little free time there has been, it's been much easier and more fun to go swimming, scooter riding and reading; anything but study! I'm going to have to knuckle down soon because it is becoming a choice between discipline and depression.

June 7, 1966
NhaTrang

Dear folks,

This is a miserable way to spend my one day off this week. I'm in bed, sick with fever, joint pains, headache, and body rash. These are all symptoms of dengue fever, a mosquito-borne tropical disease which is not too serious but darned uncomfortable for four to seven days. My misery has company, however, because Carl is sick, too. I'm afraid he is worse off than I am because his temperature is higher. About all we can do is take aspirin, drink fluids, and sleep it off. But in the meantime, it's misery. I didn't know before that I had so many joints. Dengue fever is also called breakbone fever and I think I know how it got that nickname.

Work seems to be going a little better now that we divided up the responsibilities more clearly. Marcy is in charge of the clinic; Emma is responsible for surgery, and the hospital is my department.

It still gets very discouraging at times, however. For example, earlier this week a woman brought her baby in. It was two years old and weighed nine pounds! It looked like a refugee from a concentration camp. We admitted it to the hospital and began forcing fluids and a high calorie diet which the baby took eagerly, sometimes choking in its haste. The mother was most distressed with us for giving the baby just food instead of some "magic medicine" by injection or IV. She was convinced the baby was gagging and vomiting on the food. So, despite our concern, this morning she packed her meager belongings, took her living skeleton of a baby and walked out, presumably to find another doctor. She has already been to three. Within a few days she won't have to look any more because, unless she begins to feed it something, the baby will be dead.

Some of these simple people are so superstitious and so awed by the wonders of Western culture and affluence—medicines, doctors, automobiles, money—that they seem to have no concept whatsoever of the limitations and responsibilities of those wonders. If they can have a *chich thuoc* (injection) they know they will be cured of anything; so they beg for one. An I.V. is even better. If they have a car, they usually drive as if no one else had a right to be on the road. "Americans are so rich," they think. "Why should I buy rice to feed myself while I am in the hospital. The doctor is a rich American. He can feed me." I can understand why these attitudes occur but they're still hard to deal with.

I must bring this to a close before the pain in my right hand and arm and the burning in my eyes gets any worse.

June 15, 1966
NhaTrang

Dear Folks,

Which is worse—no news or bad news? Tonight I would be delighted to sell this entire country, culture and people for far less than $24 worth of glass beads! This has been a horrible week. The fever and joint pains I had when I wrote last week are gone but the fatigue still remains. It's like nothing I've ever known before and it gets worse as the weather gets hotter. I was the first to get sick last week but, since then, nobody has felt really good; diarrhea has settled in on several of us, and short tempers are a side effect. Our unit personnel are less than perfect angels at best and this week has been miserable.

I must admit I haven't helped the situation at all. I still have to sleep an hour or two in the afternoon just to get through a "normal" day and lately our days haven't been normal. Patient census is high and there have been quite a few difficult and discouraging surgical cases lately. Last Sunday was so bad, all three of us (three times the usual number) and Doc had to work all day eight a.m. to eight p.m. with barely time off for meals! Of course everything takes at least twice as long as normal to do because of the lack of equipment and the need to hunt up an interpreter.

Seventy-five percent of the problems in the hospital which frustrate me are related to my lack of language skills. So I engaged an instructor in the hope of making a concentrated attack on the problem. However, the only hour of the day consistently free for language study is six a.m. and there goes another hour of precious sleep. In my fatigue, my language ability has gotten markedly worse.

This is what I meant by "bad news." Tonight all I can see are frustration, failure, discouragement, and fatigue. The problems seem insurmountable and innumerable! The only redeeming factors are the calm sea, beautiful mountains, lovely moonrise, and a comfortable bed to which I am going immediately. This must be what so many people meant when they said to me before I came, "It's going to be hard." I thought they meant the war!

P.S. It really helps to set all these problems down on paper and send them away!

June 22, 1966
NhaTrang

Dear Family,
    If this letter reaches you, I will be a little surprised. Our mail service has gone from bad to worse. We heard earlier this week that the director of the NhaTrang post office has been permanently transferred to Danang because he was involved in too many political activities here. So, no doubt, our poor post office is trying to break in a new director. The last letter took only eight days to get here but several others took between fifteen and thirty days. I think I shall soon send a letter out A.P.O. (military mail) just to make sure.
    Considering the general situation in this country, we know amazingly little about it since we have no newspaper and very poor radio reception. We have, however, had amazingly little political activity. NhaTrang is not strategically important to the Buddhists. Their current move is toward Saigon in order to put pressure directly on Ky's government at its capital. So we have had only about two demonstrations since I arrived, both of only minor importance. Two and a half weeks ago, however, a young Buddhist nun burned herself to death here in town. Several days later there was quite an extensive assemblage to escort her body to the cemetery which happens to be on the hill behind the hospital and one of our nurses got hung up in the traffic.
    Last Sunday night, on our way from church to dinner, we got stuck for a half hour in the traffic observing a parade. There were about a hundred Vietnamese soldiers with burning torches and various military vehicles celebrating Armed Forces Day. This seems to be an invention of Premier Ky to stir up popular support for the celebration of his first anniver-say as Premier.

It was interesting to observe the surrounding crowd as we sat watching the parade. There simply was no reaction at all, pro or con, to the marching soldiers and some of the people even looked pretty bored. My thoughts were that this would have been, strategically and psychologically, a good time for a little V.C. terrorist activity. But the evening was uneventful except for a flare, part of the celebration, which nearly fell in the middle of our dinner table as we were eating on the upstairs porch of a restaurant in town! With all that chaos in town, it was good to get home to our peace and quiet.

Work is going a little better than it was for awhile, primarily because I'm feeling better. I am still getting frustrated at my lack of ability in *tieng Viet* (Vietnamese language) but I am making a noble effort to study in my free time.

June 28, 1966
NhaTrang

Dear Sisters,

Thanks for your letter; it was one of the brighter spots of this week and one of the few communications with the outside world that have gotten through recently. That letter from you and one from Daddy containing the pictures I ordered are the only letters I have received this week. His letter was sent by mistake to Teipei, Taiwan, but I'm not sure lack of mail is entirely due to our faulty mail system. Perhaps other people are as short of letter-writing time as I am. But even this lovely, peaceful spot gets a little lonely without a few rays of life from the outside. Although the letters from my family seem to be arriving and all accounted for, I may soon send out a letter or two APO just to make sure.

I'm happy to report that within this past week's time, I had a grand total of three good days as opposed to only two that were really bad which leaves me with a positive psychological balance. Maybe that means that I'm getting a little adjusted to this confusing culture and language. Then, too, it may be because this was the week in which I had two days off instead of one!

I've been faring a little better with the language this week. Perhaps my three day a week, six to seven a.m. language study is beginning to pay off. I hope so, because I'd sure hate to think of all those good hours of sleep wasted for nothing.

For example, Friday was a good day. We were not so busy that I couldn't take the time to stand and think through what I wanted to say and how to phrase it in my limited vocabulary so I talked to my staff and the patients almost entirely in Vietnamese. Of course, there's nothing like the struggle with a foreign language to make a loquacious person suddenly become taciturn so you must realize that I don't do quite as much chattering in Vietnamese as I usually do in English!

Whether we are busy or not, however, I always take an interpreter and make my patient rounds in English. I'm all right if the patient's symptoms are confined to vomiting, diarrhea, and pain but when we get into such things as indigestion and ringing in the ears, I'm stuck. Also, it's nearly impossible for me to understand some of the older people and children because often they do not speak clearly. Refugees from the northern provinces speak a dialect I am not familiar with, which complicates matters, too. There are several hours of the day when there is no other English-speaking person in the hospital. It is truly amazing how much we can all understand of each other's speech at these times!

I'm beginning to suspect that keeping my sense of humor and being able to laugh at myself may be as important as language skills. One afternoon, earlier this week, during those hours without an interpreter, I tried to explain a procedure to one of the patients myself. I bravely started out, "Perhaps you . . . ," only to have one of the Vietnamese nurses interrupt me and finish the instructions herself. Later, she sweetly explained to me that, instead of saying, *Co le . . .* (perhaps), I had said, *Co lai . . .* (you have worms). The patient was too polite to laugh at me. But we certainly had a good chuckle over it.

Sunday was a good day, too. This was my week to have Sunday off. But, besides that, we were invited to a Vietnamese wedding. It was held at eleven a.m. after the church service in the near-by Protestant (Tin-Lanh) church where most of our Vietnamese staff attend. I attended worship service there and the bride's father gave the sermon. He is a Vietnamese missionary to Laos. After church, Doc and Carl joined me for the wedding because Emma and Marcy had to work. I can't exactly say "they joined me" because in the Tin-Lanh church, the men sit on one side of the church and the women on the other side. I sat with a couple of the staff members from the hospital and so had a running commentary, in semi-whispered Vietnamese, on what was going on.

The groom was one of Marcy's early language teachers and that, with our positions on the staff of a nearby church institution, was the reason for our invitation to the wedding. We were also invited to the wedding feast which was a fine eight-course dinner held in the yard of the home of the bride's grandmother under the shade of a parachute strung across several trees.

In proper Vietnamese society, as I understand it, the parents still sometimes do much of the business of choosing a mate for their child. However, nowadays, the children have much more of a say in the affair than they used to. This wedding was no exception, I understand. Because the parents of both bride and groom are such important people in the church, it was probably the "wedding of the year" for the church and it was truly lovely. I ventured nearly half a roll of film on the affair.

Perhaps I have mentioned before a fellow from my BVS unit, Bruce Holderread, who came to Vietnam with International Voluntary Service (IVS). His IVS project assignment was in agricultural work at BaoLoc. BaoLoc is west from here near the Laotian border in the tea growing area. Well, about a week or two after he arrived there, military activity began to pick up and the first of this week there was a battle less than two miles outside of town in which forty VC, forty ARVN (South Vietnamese regulars), and one American advisor were killed and another American and several Vietnamese were wounded. Needless to say the IVSers were evacuated here to NhaTrang. He has been out to the clinic several times and it is good to see him again.

The director of IVS in NhaTrang, Gene Stoltzfus, is a Mennonite and we have learned from him that there is a rather large battle currently being waged near Tuy Hoa, not far inland from here. It's been a destructive battle to both sides, the American casualties being flown into Eighth Field Hospital here in NhaTrang. To stand and fight a "set-piece" battle or a long-term encounter in one fixed position is a deviation from the usual Viet Cong method of operation. Their method is usually hit-and-run guerrilla warfare. However, I have heard from reasonably reliable sources that due to a recent series of VC set-backs in the war there has been a sudden large influx of troops from the North to wage these fixed battles in hopes that victory would be a morale booster to the VC troops.

Time magazine, June 17 issue with Gen. Giap on the cover, would have you believe that the war is nearly won. It's a little hard to be that optimistic here in the midst of all three of the Vietnamese wars: military, economic, and political.

Ah well, I guess I shall leave politics and war to the politicians and generals and stick to nursing. That is a full-time job just now. Last night a baby died of encephalitis or meningitis. Today another one is dying and the mother tells us that there are many sick children in her village. Just like her boy, they have a high fever and no other symptoms. We're somewhat baffled by the organism, and with no lab facilities, we have no way of isolating it.

The children both came in with very high fevers, 106 and 105. They had had fever for about two weeks but they had no other symptoms and were alert, talking and able to drink. We started them both on penicillin and sulfadiazine IV which is treatment for encephalitis and their fevers came down. But, within a few hours, they became comatose and began having abnormal muscle movements, convulsions, and then died. It's almost as if the causative organism feeds on penicillin. That is entirely possible because the province nurses give a large shot of penicillin to anybody who comes in with the slightest complaint. Some of the people build up a great tolerance to the antibiotic, so there's no reason to believe that the germs don't. Today another child came in with a high fever. I hope we have better luck this time. It sure gets discouraging.

Well, I must go—there's so much to be done on that one day off and the time goes so fast!

June 28, 1966
NhaTrang

Dear Folks,

Well, since we have all gotten over our major illnesses, we have been bothered by a rash of minor illnesses such as boils, tropical ulcers, jelly fish stings and, for me, an epidemic of insect bites and stings. I look like I have the measles and I have this charming little morning and night ritual of sitting on the edge of the bed scratching for about fifteen minutes before I can get up or go to sleep. I don't know what I've been bitten by but no self-respecting mosquito would bite me in some of the places I have welts! Doc says that I must have body lice, which wouldn't be impossible around some of these places and people.

Well, I realize that this doesn't say too much. I didn't intend to. I just wanted to make sure that a letter gets out letting you know that I am well, happy, safe and working hard. With renewed and increased military action around Tuy Hoa and BaoLoc, I can just imagine what the newspapers are reporting. But don't worry; we have more peace and quiet here at the clinic than you do there at the farm. I wish you could be here to enjoy it.

I'm not quite sure how this letter will get out. Carl has made friends with one of the GIs who works at Eighth Field Hospital and he has said we can use this APO number if we want to. But I want to ask him first. I thought he'd be out today but he wasn't. So it may be delayed a few days until I can ask his permission.

July 9, 1966
NhaTrang

Dear Friends,

Every day it gets harder and harder to find time to sit down and write this letter; and, believe it or not, I find it harder and harder to find anything to say. Life has become a routine of daily work, days off, trips to town or the beach. Then I remember that just because it is no longer so new and different to me does not mean that it may not be interesting to you. In fact, a recitation of my daily or weekly routine would give you a far better picture of the "whats and whys" of my being here than my telling you about the special events gripping this nation. That you can read about in the newspaper.

Since I arrived here at NhaTrang the first of May, we have organized a division of labor among the three nurses. Marcy, a twenty-two year old Canadian nurse is in charge of the outpatient clinic five days a week. Emma, also a Canadian with many years experience in delivery room and operating room nursing, is in charge of surgery on Wednesdays and Saturdays and she assists in the clinic on nonsurgery days. That leaves me with the hospital.

That's not as big or important a job as it sounds. We seldom have more than fifty or less than thirty patients in our thirty-three beds. Since the hospital is already about ten years old, the organization and routines of care are well established. So my work is simply the administration of nursing care to the inpatients: passing medications, noting and carrying out doctor's orders, giving baths, doing treatments, making rounds, supervision of other nursing staff and assisting the doctor with treatments as needed. This is the kind of job many of you are familiar with and may now be engaged in.

We have a fine Vietnamese staff of five young women in the hospital. There are three young women and three men working in the clinic. The men also take their turns in the hospital for evenings, nights, and weekends. The staff give medications and supposedly do treatments and baths. That sounds like it doesn't leave much for me to do, doesn't it?

Well, some days it seems like I don't do very much except to mix the milk which we give the patients twice daily as a dietary supplement and make morning rounds with my interpreter. Then there are other days when, on my way to the hospital at eight a.m., I am greeted at the door by three staff members, all talking at once. *Cai thuoc het roi* (This medicine is all gone). *Xin di thay ong a-sau, co mua* (Please see the man in bed A-6. He is vomiting). *Cai em-be co sot hai ba ngay roi* (This baby has had a fever for two or three days).

I turn around to see two clinic patients standing there also waiting for me. If it is a clinic day I send them back to clinic without even listening to their complaints. For, just like patients in clinics all over the States, they thought perhaps they could avoid the waiting back in the clinic by coming into the hospital and trying out my sympathetic ear. What they don't know is that if their temperature is under 102, my ear is not very sympathetic!

If it is not a clinic day, I must interview them, write up their symptoms and decide if and when to call the doctor to see them or to admit them to the hospital. That isn't too hard except that right now my interpreter is on vacation. So what happens is that I question the patient in my very poor Vietnamese. One of my staff translates it into good Vietnamese and then translates the patient's answer back into my rudimentary vocabulary. We not only interview patients like this, we make rounds like this! The patients get quite a laugh out of it and I've learned more Vietnamese this week without an interpreter than I did the two months before with one!

By the time I've answered these questions and gotten these problems solved, it is already nine o'clock and I haven't yet sat down at the desk to organize the day. About the time I start to check the agenda book for the day or the temperature book, one of the Vietnamese nurses comes in and says, *Co, ong o phong kia co mau nhieu,* (The man on the porch is having much bleeding). He was having abdominal pain and distention due to liver damage, decreased bowel tone and general poor condition. Since it wasn't getting better fast enough with our doctor's medicine, the family decided to take matters into their own hands. According to the custom of Vietnamese "medicine," a series of parallel cuts is made with a sharp object over the painful part, just deep enough so it will bleed and "let the pain out." This man's wife had made several small cuts across his abdomen and, due to a prothrombin deficiency with his hepatitis, the bleeding was persistent.

We took him into the operating room and put sutures in the largest of the cuts. Then we moved him into the hospital where he could be observed more closely. Due to his generally poor condition and unwillingness to drink fluids, the doctor ordered an IV started on him. By the time I got that mixed and started, sitting on the floor in the dark corner of the back ward, another hour is gone.

Admissions continue to come in from the clinic. As beds fill up, I begin to look for places on the porch or the floor in the hall where we can put a mat for the next one.

A patient comes in from the TB house to tell me that another patient out there is coughing up blood. Of course I go out to check him. He doesn't have very much blood in his sputum and his pulse and blood pressure are all right. However, all of the TB patients are understandably frightened at the slightest trace of blood in their sputum. So I try to reassure him, give him the usual medicines and tell him to breathe shallowly, try not to cough, and rest. At least that's what I try to tell him!

By this time I've given up trying to organize the day and decide to just try to survive it instead. I help the cleaning woman carry out the trash and dirty laundry because it's too heavy for her alone and the Vietnamese girls are too small to help.

I get the Vietnamese nurses started on washing windows or cleaning out cupboards in their spare time by doing a few myself. I have to check with them specifically about any job I want done, explain as carefully as possible how to do it, perhaps demonstrate and then ask or observe to see that it is done. Only two of the girls have had any nursing training at all and much of that consisted of treatments and procedures such as giving medications, starting IV's, attending women in labor and similar tasks. So, such things as baths, forcing fluids and back care must be taught when the situation arises. That, too, is time-consuming when one must look up the meaning of every other word needed to explain.

Actually, considering the age and limited training of these girls, they do very well. We are hoping, however, to soon set up nurses' training classes here at the hospital to educate our present staff. If we can get government recognition we will be able to provide training for other girls interested in nursing as a career.

Rounds are the best part of my day in the hospital, especially now that I have to work almost all of the time without an interpreter. I go from patient to patient, observing their condition, listening to (and usually not understanding) their complaints, giving medication as needed and ordered, and try to explain a little of what is going on with their disease and therapy. This is my closest and most prolonged contact with the patients and their families all day. It is my opportunity to communicate with them verbally (but more often otherwise) my concern, care instructions, and the availability of myself and the rest of the staff to help them. I'm afraid that upon frequent occasions I also communicate irritation.

I am trying to instruct the wife of the man with the cut belly to give him fluids to drink after I have catheterized him for only ten cc of urine. The urine was the color and consistency of pancake syrup because his kidneys are rapidly on the way to shutting down. She says, "But he doesn't want to drink." *Irritation.*

I ask the mother of a feverish child why she keeps removing the cold wet towels with which we have been sponging him. She replies, "But he has a fever." *Irritation.*

A TB patient asks for the tenth day in a row for a *chich thuoc* (injection of medication) because he is *met qua*. There is simply no adequate English translation of this phrase. Roughly translated, it means "extremely tired" and it seems to be the Vietnamese national disease. *Irritation.*

Another patient asks for rice, the twentieth such request for the day. Not that he really needs it but he has heard his neighbor say that the doctor has rice to give away. *Irritation.*

But about that time the family member of a patient shyly comes into the nurses' station carrying a tray on which are perhaps some bananas, some mangosteens, some cactus fruit or a few eggs (and it was once two live ducks!) She hands it to one of us and says, *Xin cho Bac-si va noi cam on* (Please give this to the doctor and tell him thank you.)

Sometimes it is just watching three or four children who were feverish a few days earlier playing together and laughing. Or to see a patient's face light up as he tells you how well he can see out of an eye from which the doctor removed a cataract. Then the irritation melts and I'm ready for a few more hours of the battle!

I guess I could ramble on about work for quite a while but that's not all life here consists of either. All of us at the hospital work hard and put in long hours. But we are not interested in becoming martyrs to the place so we all get in a fair share of recreation, too. The sea is less than two hundred yards from our front door and there is a good swimming beach only a five minute walk away which gets much use from all of us.

We even own a boat, the Buu-Tin. Translated, her name means Faith and I think that's what she sails on. She is temporarily in dry dock for repairs but when she is ship-shape again and the hospital is quiet on a weekend, some of us will go sailing to a nearby island.

We eat out every Sunday night and go into Nha Trang frequently for errands, sodas or ice cream. All of us have friends in the community, both American and Vietnamese, so we often have more guests and visiting than we know what to do with. Tomorrow, those of us who are not working plan to go sailing in a rented boat and take a picnic dinner. The other night we went into Nha Trang for American-style hamburgers and ice cream. That was my first since I left the States four and a half months ago. They really tasted good!

So, sometimes as I take an hour off work to go swimming, spend my day off scootering around Nha Trang or entertaining friends, it is hard for me to remember that this is volunteer service and not a vacation. But there are other times, like last week. The hospital was extremely busy: I couldn't understand anything any Vietnamese said to me and they couldn't understand me. The patients needed things we didn't have. I had diarrhea about twenty times a day. The temperature was a humid 110 degrees. I'd gotten up three times the night before to check on patients. At times like that, this seems more like a test of my endurance than volunteer service! But, then, what is healthful living anyway but finding a balance between endurance and enjoyment? Most days I can find it.

This schedule of our daily life is little affected by the political and military events which you read and hear about every day. Two weeks ago the country celebrated Armed Forces Day. This was proclaimed a national holiday by Premier Ky, some would say to celebrate the anniversary of his first year in office. Emma and I were in town that evening and got caught in the traffic jam created by the parade of torch-bearing soldiers marching down main street.

The recent large scale battle in TuyHoa increased the daily number of helicopters flying over our house as they were ferrying casualties to Eighth Field Hospital in NhaTrang. The X-ray department at the hospital there was so busy with these casualties that we had to wait an hour or two to get our few TB patients checked.

Our mail service has gotten progressively slower and slower because the director of the post office here in Nha-Trang was permanently transferred to Danang. Rumor has it that he was involved in too much political activity here. And yesterday we learned by rumor (apparently the most rapid and reliable means of communication in this country) that all Air Vietnam commercial flights for the month of July have been suspended. Because of the food shortage in Hue, even commercial planes must be pressed into service carrying food to that region. That means no mail in or out as it all travels by air. Road transport is entirely unreliable. I hope the rumor is false but we'll soon find out!

Incoming patients sometimes mention military action inland. The Vietnamese noncommissioned officers' academy just a mile or two down the beach from us goes literally full-blast day and night with training exercises. There are artillery practice, tracer bullets and flares, parachute practice, troop landings on our swimming beach, and other similar activities. Only in these ways are we here at the clinic reminded of the war around us.

I sometimes even find myself forgetting about the war altogether until I am jarred back to reality by some specific reminder. As we scootered along the road one day last week, we saw a man trudging along in his black pajama suit heavily armed with a rifle, sidearms and a full ammunition belt. We passed with caution, I assure you, but as I smiled at him he returned the smile and nodded pleasantly. War has to be fought by machines—human machines and mechanical machines. It could never be successfully waged by persons!

Well, my friends, you are very often in my thoughts. Please be patient with unanswered letters. Shortage of time and unreliability of mail service make good excuses but I am trying to answer them all. You are remembered in my prayers as I hope I am in yours.

P.S. I must add a note about Sunday. We went snorkeling off the coast of an island out in NhaTrang Bay. I had never been snorkeling before but after I learned how to breathe properly through the snorkel and how to keep the face mask from steaming up, they could hardly get me to come up to the terrestrial world again. It was like swimming around in my own private aquarium. The view was indescribably beautiful with live coral, sea anemones, purple star fishes, sea urchins, sponges, pink jelly fish and about twenty kinds of tropical fish of every imaginable color. After five hours in the sun, we were an unimaginable color, too, by the time we got home! But it was a glorious experience.

6
In Leisure Time

Newsweek
June 27, 1966

The Gut Issue

Though it is the struggle between the Buddhists and the generals that dominates the headlines out of Vietnam, the Vietnamese man in the street is far more concerned with another issue: the cost of living. And not without reason—for inflation in Vietnam has now reached the point where it threatens the entire social and economic fabric of the nation.

Since January 1965, retail food prices in Saigon have soared by 74 percent, and the overall cost of living has jumped 70 percent in the same period. Hardest hit have been Vietnam's civil servants. Long accustomed to special status and privilege, they have watched their incomes, which remained unchanged, steadily dwindle in purchasing power while cabbies, landlords and bar girls who fatten on free-spending GIs have become the new elite. In desperation, many middle-level civil servants have quit the government to work for the Americans. Typical is Dang Tran Luong, 38, who left a $150-a-month government post for a clerk's job with a U.S. company. "My government salary only lasted for the first ten days of the month," he said, "instead of for the entire month, as it did before."

One result of this has been a steady deterioration of South Vietnam's public services. A Saigon garbage collector, for example, makes about 75 cents a day, but he can earn more than twice that with a U.S. contractor. As a result, Saigon now has only 70 garbagemen where it used to have 300, and heaps of ripe, runny garbage offend eyes and noses all over the capital.

.... But last week [Premier Nguyen Cao] Ky finally acted. Up went salaries for the military and civil servants (increases range from 20 to 30 per cent). Down went the South Vietnamese piaster, devalued from an official rate of 35 to $1 to 80 to $1, with a "special addition" that fixed the effective rate at 118 to $1. (Last week's black-market rate: 180 to $1.) And on top of all this, Ky established a free market in gold, to force down the piaster's black-market price. (About $4.4 million worth of gold was smuggled in from Laos last year for sale to anxious Vietnamese.

These were steps in the right direction, but they did not strike at the basic causes of the inflation, one of which is the fact that the Saigon government is spending far beyond its income. . . .

Still more damaging than government spending, however, is the fact that the U.S. is pouring indigestible amounts of money into the South Vietnamese economy, partly through crash construction programs which have absorbed enormous amounts of labor and partly through the spending of GIs intent on forgetting the war, however expensively. . . .

In short, while the measures that Ky took last week might ameliorate his country's economic distress, they could not cure it. That, unhappily, could only be accomplished by one thing: an end to the Vietnamese war.

July 20, 1966
NhaTrang

Dear Folks,

Where does the time go? It must have been two weeks since I've written though I can't imagine where those weeks have gone without my knowing. Last week our patient census got down to about thirty-five and Marcy kept saying, "I wish we'd get some patients in; I don't like it when it's quiet like this." Well, this week she's gone to Saigon for a month of language study and we have about fifty patients, several of them quite sick! Due to this and a few extra-curricular activities such as going to a movie, a Sunday afternoon scenic drive, taking people into town to meet early morning planes, and six a.m. language study, I'm using almost every free minute to catch up on sleep. I've almost forgotten how it feels not to be tired and my good humor suffers so much with fatigue.

Yesterday on my day off I had a new and interesting experience. I went village visiting with one of the Wycliffe Bible Translators' missionaries who works among the Roglai tribe. We went to a small village of Roglai people about thirty to thirty-five kilometers south and west of NhaTrang.

The population of Vietnam is made up of two distinct types of people: the Vietnamese or Annamese who live in the coastal plains, and the tribes people or Montagnards who live in the interior mountainous regions of the country. The mountains comprise more than seventy-five percent of the total area of the country but they are inhabited by only about one million tribes people as opposed to the fifteen million Vietnamese on the coastal plains. There are about forty-five different tribes, the Roglai being one of them.

Each tribe speaks a different language; all quite different from Vietnamese. The tribes people vary somewhat in physical characteristics but they are uniformly distinguishable from the Vietnamese by their darker skins, rounder eyes, and stockier stature. The relationship between the two peoples is in many ways similar to the black-white relationship in the States a decade ago, i.e., complete separation which keeps one race inferior to the other. The Montagnards are often referred to by the Vietnamese as *moi* (savages) and are discriminated against in many ways.

We visited a small Roglai village of about forty houses. I had taken along a bag of medicines and bandages and held informal clinic, dispensing pills and advice. I must have seen and talked with about twenty-five to thirty people whose symptoms ranged from "dying two times last night," through "shaking in the stomach" and "hit by a tree" to "skinny." Between my silent prayers for guidance as to what to say or do, I cursed myself silently for being such a fake, handing out aspirins and cough syrup for what might well be malaria and tuberculosis. But these people are unbelievably poor and quite remote from medical care so maybe even aspirin and cough syrup are better than nothing at all. I took a few pictures of the people and the village which are not yet developed but the weather was not very cooperative with picture-taking.

To top off the day, on the way to the village we came upon the scene of an accident. An American army truck, loaded with GIs, had hit a Vietnamese-driven construction company truck. I suspect that, as usual, they were both going too fast. One Vietnamese was hurt pretty badly, so we stopped and I surveyed his injuries. There wasn't a medic on the scene yet and I had no idea how to start giving first aid without even water! By the time I started to clean him up with somebody's T-shirt wet down from a canteen, a Korean medic arrived. He knew much more about what to do than I did. So we pooled ignorances, washed and bandaged as much as we could without moving the patient and then waited for the ambulance to come. After they loaded him, the medic disappeared. I tried to, too, but the police were using our vehicle for a writing desk. So, I couldn't slip away till I gave my name and address. I hope I don't get a military court summons!

Well, mornings come early and lately not too "bright with do," so I'd better get to bed before too late.

July 25, 1966
NhaTrang

Dear Sisters,

I trust the folks share letters with you so I won't repeat my account of my visit to the tribe's village last week. It's just about the last interesting and exciting thing that has happened to me for quite awhile. Except, of course, for an unpacifistically angry outburst at a couple of half-drunk fighter pilots last night while we were eating out. But such is life for an American woman in the war zone!

Things have been so quiet around here for a few weeks that it's almost hard to find anything to write about. Marcy has gone to Saigon for a month of language study and we've been joined by another nurse. Her main job is to begin setting up a nurses training program at the clinic. It is a terribly slow process to develop such a program from scratch since every endeavor takes three times as long as one expects. So the training program will probably still be in the planning stages long after I leave to come home.

Oh, I must share with you one funny thing that happened to me this week. I learned why the Vietnamese nurses wear white satin pants *(quan)* under their uniform dresses.

I was making rounds the other morning, checking on several patients who had had eye surgery the day before. One was a young mother who had brought her little son, about two years old, to stay with her at the hospital. As I bent over to change the dressing on his mother's eye, he was fascinated by the sight of my bare legs sticking out from under my uniform skirt. He had probably never seen bare female legs before, so he decided to investigate further. He simply lifted the back of my full uniform skirt up over his head, walked inside and looked around! The patients were too polite to laugh but the nurses couldn't suppress a giggle.

Needless to say, I came back to work after the afternoon siesta wearing *quan* under my uniform dress! I've found the pants also help keep the flies off the insect bites and skin ulcers on my legs. Maybe they'll finally heal.

I think of you all so often and sometimes get a little homesick to see you.

August 3, 1966
NhaTrang

Dear Folks,

How I wish I could sit down and chat with you a little while right now. There are so many things on my mind that I want to tell you and ask you. Most of them are unimportant little details that are hard to write about so this letter will probably be largely incoherent.

Please convey my thanks to all those people from whom I've received such kind letters and have not yet answered. I appreciate them so much but I've just about given up trying to answer all of them. The GI whose APO number I used to send a letter and several rolls of film out to you was out here yesterday to take me for a scooter ride. He had dinner with us and said his final good-byes. He left for the States early this a.m. for discharge from the Army. While he was here yesterday, he showed me the letter you had written him. He appreciated it and may answer if he gets the chance.

Last week I received from the denominational offices a copy of the new contract of service recently drawn up specifically for those of us serving in Vietnam. It raised the monthly allowance from ten dollars to thirty dollars, cutting out vacation allowance. Other provisions are the same except that on my contract the term of service was listed as twenty-four consecutive months.

After some thought, I wrote back to them returning the contract and asking that the terms of my old contract be renewed. That contract provided for an allowance of ten dollars per month and a term of at least twelve consecutive months. As I explained, I do not work well in a situation where verbal communication has as many barriers as it does here and my frustration level gets pretty high quite often. Therefore, I am not sure if my limited effectiveness in this situation would warrant my staying two years even if my frustration level would allow it.

Increasingly, for the past few weeks, I've been subject to a sense of disappointment in myself and the work I am doing. The most basic and obvious failure I find in myself is my language ability. I am making progress but painfully slowly and I am so far from being conversant in Vietnamese as to be laughable. Right now I am not even motivated to study as much as I should. Often I don't even feel like practicing what I do know. I use the excuse of fatigue, and indeed I often fall asleep over my Vietnamese book. But even this is sometimes a defense mechanism, I am sure.

Secondly, and perhaps more importantly, I am supposedly working here as an instrument of Christian love. As a matter of fact, however, for the past three months, more often than not, I have been neither Christian nor loving. Never before have I known myself to become frustrated and angry so often and so easily. Many are the days in which I do not even like these people, let alone love them. How can I love persons when there is no communication and I can't do anything for them or give them what they want? That is so often the case here which creates frustration and leads to anger. Result? My hypocritical Christian witness.

I'm wondering more every day what God is asking of me. If I am attempting to do what is right, why am I not given the strength to react to these frustrations with love? On the other hand, perhaps expectations that are not met are Mary Sue's, not God's. I don't know but, as I look at the examples of my coworkers, I often feel more of a liability than an asset.

Well, so much for crying in my tea. There's always tomorrow to try to redeem myself, and so I shall. I wouldn't come home right now if I got a return trip ticket free of charge. I want to be able to feel good about this place and my work when I come home and, as the Vietnamese say, *chua duoc* (not yet). As always, I can say with assurance, I know that I will survive. But will I be able to carry out my responsibility to other people in the meantime?

Don't let me worry you. I'm not exactly despondent. I simply have to get some of these feelings out of my system. I dare not burden people here with them, because they are subject to the same frustrations as I am.

I will write to my sisters again when I am in a better humor. And I probably will be by the time you get this letter. Take care of yourselves. From the news reports we hear here. Vietnam is safer right now than many of the big cities in the States. Elections for the National Assembly in Saigon are approaching. It will be the first elected government for this country in twelve years. Perhaps this will give the news reporters something besides war news to report. We here at the clinic are sitting tight, waiting and keeping an ear to the ground. Elections are a promising step both in political and military progress but they are going to be fraught with difficulties.

August 9, 1966
NhaTrang

Dear Sisters,

The past month has fairly flown by as we've been very busy. The patient census is high: forty-five to fifty-five in our thirty-three beds. Daily clinics have been large and surgery schedule has been heavy. Various staff members, both stateside and Vietnamese, have been off on vacations or sick.

Finally, for the last two weeks, our cook, (who also does our ironing and supervises the laundry) took a long-awaited vacation. Now, mind you, I'm not complaining. However, every time I dash from work to the kitchen to start lunch or I spend my one day a week off ironing, I decide more firmly that I'm not the dual-career type person. It's got to be either nursing or housekeeping, but not both! Unfortunately, these past two nights it has been my turn to fix supper. The cuts of meat that the house girl called *thit bo* or cow meat turned out to be water buffalo instead of beef. And it must have been an old one at that! The dogs ate well but tonight again we're filling up on cookies. I'm sure we won't starve until the cook gets back next week but it's been a trial for Doc's appetite and a boon to his subtle humor.

This afternoon our second doctor, Dr. Harold Kraybill, arrived with his wife, Esther. They are a Mennonite couple about my age or a little less. He is from Pennsylvania and she from Virginia. It will be nice to have another doctor around here to get the work done but it will put a cramp on our living quarters.

New people joining our unit have much to get used to. Besides the six human members of the unit, there are our pets, two dogs and a gecko. A gecko is a lizard, gray-blue in color with red, measle-like spots and bright beady eyes. Geckoes catch and eat mosquitoes and other insects. Ours is about a foot and a half long and lives underneath the picture on the dining room wall.

Usually, as we eat supper, he silently creeps out from behind the picture and up the wall to dine on the insects attracted by the florescent light above. As he eats, he is in full view of those seated around three sides of our dining room table.

I had forgotten all about him until last night at supper when I was reminded again by the wide-eyed look on the face of the new doctor's wife. I tried not to laugh at her reaction, or to feel smug at being such an "old hand" at cultural adjustment!

Two of us went for an evening swim tonight before the moon was up. It was truly lovely because the water was full of a certain kind of algae which gives off a phosphorescent glow at night when the water is disturbed. As we walked or swam through the water, it looked as if all the stars had fallen into the sea. Sights like this go a long way in preparing me to meet the frustrations of the coming day.

Well, it's way past bedtime. Tomorrow comes early and last night was so late!

August 10, 1966
NhaTrang

Dear Family,

Two letters off to you in two days! I'm going to have to resort to carbon paper soon or lose contact with some of you. I've not heard from any of my BVS unit for over three months; it's been about that long since I've heard from any of my college or nursing school friends. In fact, letters from my family are doubly important because they're the only ones I can count on with regularity any more.

Tonight, right after supper, I was so tired I went to bed for a few hours. In my dozing, half-wakeful state, I dreamed of ice cream, family holidays, hot showers, and freedom from mosquitoes! I guess that's homesickness.

I don't know where the time has gone this past month. We certainly haven't been sitting around with time to commiserate. Business continues as usual. There have been a hundred to 180 patients a day in clinic, and surgery has been running all morning and all afternoon besides. The patient census has been fifty or more in our thirty-three hospital beds with three patients in the hall on the floor, three in the lab room on the floor, and seven on the porch on mats on the floor.

August 14, 1966

Here I sit, falling asleep over this letter again but I'm determined to get if off to you before another day is gone. I think that both physically and emotionally I'm not cut out for this kind of life. There are a few too many endemic diseases to which I'm susceptible and too much hard work and long hours which never did agree with my congenital laziness. But, by far the worst, is my reaction to the many frustrations inherent in a situation like this. Why should I repeat what I've said so many times before? By now you must think I'm headed for a psychotic break! Well, I'm not 'cause I'm too stubborn. But the frustration and depression continue. Oh, well, maybe I'll get adjusted by the time to come home!

August 15, 1966
NhaTrang

Dear Folks,

It's late. I'm tired and must turn in soon. Marcy got back from a month of language study in Saigon so there are now four nurses and two doctors here. Our Saigon office has suggested I should take a few days off this week and come down there for a rest.

We have a patient who needs to be escorted back to Pleiku. So, I will leave here for Pleiku about ten a.m. tomorrow morning. I'll stay there for a few days, visit some of our other Vietnam Christian Service workers who are stationed there. Then I plan to go on down to Saigon for a few days of visiting.

I've not done much traveling in Vietnam yet, partly because travel schedules are so uncertain as to be laughable. Last Saturday, Emma spent the entire day on a plane to Pleiku and never got there. She went instead to Saigon, Kontum, Ankhe and QuinNhon! That's not at all unusual. A traveller here may have to spend an entire day in an airport somewhere waiting for a flight to their chosen destination.

Accommodations when traveling are also unpredictable. We women are warned rather sternly by the men of our unit that if we are stranded overnight when traveling, we are not to go to a hotel. We are to sleep in the airport or seek out a missionary's home. I'll spare you their explanations in graphic detail, but it sounds as if they are trying to protect more than just our reputations!

Therefore, I haven't thought traveling was worth the effort. But I don't want to come home not having seen anything of this country besides Saigon and NhaTrang. So I'd better get started.

The plane strike in the U.S. is really making a difference in our mail service. I've only received about three letters in the past two weeks. It's a rather desolate feeling but I know that I can chalk it up to the strike.

By the way, the former Saigon director of Vietnam Christian Service, Dr. Atlee Beechy, is now on his way home. He and his wife live in Goshen, Indiana, near the college campus.

I'm sure they would be delighted to have you stop in some-time. They could tell you about our work and show you some pictures. He is, without doubt, one of the finest examples of Christianity in practice that I have ever met. His presence in Vietnam was a great help to our work and to the Christian climate of our lives.

August 21, 1966
Saigon

Dear Folks,

This short vacation from work has been very good for my frame of mind. It's good, and necessary, for me to get away from work for a little while. And it is very good for me to get out and see what other workers are doing in their assignments. I know now, without a shadow of a doubt, that NhaTrang is the best place I could be and I have no desire whatsoever to trade for any other location. We usually have too much work and the resulting physical fatigue is one of the reasons it's been good for me to get away. But that is so much better a problem to have than not having enough work to do. And that is the case on a few of the other projects because of the grinding slowness of administrative work in this country.

Well, back to letter writing after a little nap. I also took time out to go to evening church service and to do a little visit-ing. Vietnam Christian Service now has about forty people in the country. About half of them are currently in Saigon in language study. That creates quite a housing problem and so, besides the center where I lived while I was in Saigon, the organization has rented at least four other houses of varying sizes in order to be able to house everybody. So, tonight, after church, we did a little visiting, and I think I have finally seen all the houses and met all the new people. It is really fascinating to see all the various shades of religious persuasion and experience we have represented within this one organi-zation.

By the way, I forgot to tell you: I have agreed to extend my term for two months until May 1, 1967. This will make exactly one year of work and I do not feel that I can count those first six weeks of orientation and language study within a year of work. So don't expect me home too soon!

Well, I must go to bed before too long. Since I am leaving for home early in the morning that means I will have to finish my public epistle after I return to NhaTrang. When I will find the time again I do not know, but I will!

P.S. My camera was stolen in Pleiku so I've ordered another one from Hong Kong. I'm glad you've deposited a little money for me!

August 25, 1966
NhaTrang

My Dear Friends,
After almost four months here at Chan-Y-Vien Tin-Lanh, I'm getting reacquainted with leisure time! Our Western staff has increased from one doctor and three nurses to two doctors, four nurses, and a housemother and hostess. So, although the work load remains about the same, it's now spread over a few more people. It seems like real luxury now, not having to do the mending, no longer having responsibility for planning entertainment for guests in addition to a day's work, and working only three evenings every two weeks. And, to top it all off, I just got back from a week's vacation to Pleiku and Saigon! In the army vacation time is called R and R: rest and recuperation. My vacation was R and R, too!

The two weeks before my vacation, our cook was on vacation and we took turns doing the cooking. Those of you who remember my cooking ability will know why I needed a vacation for recuperation! In addition to having to get accustomed to a very temperamental two burner gas stove and a charcoal burner over which I lost quite a lot of religion, I am not accustomed to the types of food available. It will be a long time, if ever, until I live down my attempt to make scrambled eggs out of dried eggs. My attempt to fix *thit bo* (literally cow meat) like beef roast or broiled steak was an even worse disaster. Both nights, as we had to employ a hacksaw to carve the meat, we decided that *thit bo* must mean water buffalo and not beef cow.

But my culinary efforts were not a complete failure because nobody died of ptomaine poisoning and it provided us with plenty of laughs, both at the time and since. I discovered that the scrambled egg story even preceded me to Saigon and people whom I hadn't even met yet were laughing over my "kitchen kapers."

There were other reasons for welcoming a little time off. Our nurse with the most seniority, who serves as our unofficial authority on all matters in the hospital and clinic, had gone to Saigon for another month of language study. The other three of us muddled but we managed to get through. However, as I think back on the month she was gone, it seems like a nightmare of fatigue, depression, frustration with the language, and with just too much plain hard work. But, in particular, I remember three patients.

The first was an elderly man, admitted with heart disease, who went progressively down hill. At first no matter how many times a day I went back to his corner of the ward for any reason at all, he would call to me. When I asked what he wanted, he would just take my hand and, with a twinkle in his eye, would say, *Manh gioi cho?*, (How are you?) It might be twenty times a day, but always there was the twinkle and the question: "How are you?"

As he got worse, it was no longer a greeting but a recitation of complaints. Then one day his speech was pretty incoherent and that night he fell out of bed several times. The next morning he looked to be only hours away from death, so one of us spent all day at his bedside. With the help of IV medications, his blood pressure came back up and by evening he was talking again.

Within a few days there was a weak reminder of that old twinkle back in his eye and once again I would hear, *Co-oi, co-oi. Manh gioi cho?* He was soon able to be up and around again but it was obvious we had saved him from death only temporarily. He died last week while I was gone. He had no family at all. I wish at least that I had been here to be with him.

The second was a lady of about forty-five or fifty. Mother of seven children, she had been sick for seven to ten days before they brought her in from quite a distance away, carry-ing her in a hammock litter. She was in profound, dehydra-tion and shock from cholera! I saw her two hours after she was admitted and in my mind I gave her little chance of living.

IV fluids are never in abundance around here but we begged, borrowed, and "stole" and really poured them into her. She was so debilitated that she began to show signs of pressure sores within twenty-four hours after arrival. (This is a constant problem since the beds have no mattresses.)

Her husband and a son came with her and stayed to care for her. For several nights, every two hours all night, whichever of us was on call went over to the hospital to regu-late the IV, turn her and try to give her fluids to drink.

Her husband was nearly sick himself with worry about her those first few nights. "Will she get better or is she going to die?" "We have seven children. What will I do if she dies?" They are Buddhists but they had been reading one of the Christian tracts passed out to the patients by the hospital chaplain and the patient's husband told me, in simple Viet-namese and with sign language, that he was praying to *Jesu Christ* for his wife's health.

It took four weeks but that woman walked out of the hos-pital yesterday and went home. Doc jokingly said that she bowed so low when she thanked him that he had to stop her before she hit her head on the floor. It took her a full five minutes to say all her thank-yous: *Cam-on Bac-si, cam-on y-ta, cam-on Chua* (Thank-you, doctor, thank-you nurses, thank-you Lord.)

The third patient I remember even more distinctly. A little eight-year-old girl was brought in with severe breathing dif-ficulty. X-ray showed a massively enlarged heart shadow. The doctor suspected pericarditis and confirmed his diagnosis by getting large amounts of pus from the pericardium, the sac around the heart. After this, her respiratory difficulty was markedly lessened and she was much improved.

On her trip to the Army hospital for X-ray she made fast friends with an Air Force man who works there. He came out to clinic to see her several times, bringing her candy and other little gifts. She reminded him so much of his daughter back home.

Her symptoms began to return and another pericardial tap revealed more pus. This time the doctor inserted penicillin into the heart sac in an attempt to kill the infection. Again she was better but not as much as before. In her weakness and respiratory decompensation, she had developed a pneumonia.

Antibiotics did not seem to be effective and we have no oxygen and no humidity tent. So, one evening, her grandmother and I sat and watched her die. How did I explain to that grandmother, in a foreign tongue, that I *did* care about her granddaughter but there was simply nothing more that we could do? I didn't! I just sat there getting more frustrated by the minute and more sick of the whole impossible situation.

After the child died, I watched her clutch that little body in her arms and wail her grief aloud to the skies for several hours. Then it was time for the old woman to take the little body home for burial. I had to tell her when she asked, "No, the doctor cannot take your child's body home in his car," (there are four bridges between here and there that have been blown by the VC). "No, the doctor cannot give you money to hire a vehicle to take the body home" (because if we did we would then automatically have to do it for everyone and we simply do not have that kind of money.)

And so, as so often happens when I am faced by an impossible situation like this, I got angry. A natural enough reaction but not exactly an asset to my Christian witness to the power of love and kindness! That's when I begin to get depressed and begin to wonder if it will ever be possible to live the principles I believe in and which prompted me to come here.

This leads to more frustration and anger, a vicious cycle which tells me, when I take the time to sit back and study it, why and how wars start. My broken relationships with people here, I think, must parallel the broken relationships between nations. Like my anger, wars spring in part from inability to communicate and find a solution to a seemingly impossible situation. It's a hard road to find on a personal level. I guess I never before knew just *how* hard. The difficulties are multiplied a hundred-fold on a national level. But I still believe it is possible to function on the power of Christian love. I've seen the results on a personal level, here and elsewhere, and I know it is the better way.

And so, after four months of waging (and pacifying) these little personal wars, struggling with the language and modifying nursing procedures almost beyond recognition on a sixty-hour-work week, I must admit I anticipated a week off. I did not anticipate traveling by air in Vietnam, however. I had not been on a plane since my trip here from Saigon four months ago. That experience of thirty minutes in the midst of a violent thunderstorm in a small two-engine, seven passenger aircraft almost cured me of air travel for all time.

But, in faith and with anticipation, I set out for Pleiku on Tuesday morning. Doc went along after much arm-twisting, mostly, I think, to carry my suitcase which contained, among other things, about fifteen pounds of potatoes which we were donating to the Pleiku unit from our surplus! We had a lovely flight and, since Pleiku is in the mountains and is in the midst of its rainy season, we stepped from the plane into the first "cold" weather I've found since I've come to this country; all of seventy degrees!

At Pleiku I was able to renew some old acquaintances. The two fellows who traveled from the States with me are working there and I had not seen them since we all had left Saigon. Rufus, from Virginia, is working on an experimental farm owned by the provincial government which is used to demonstrate and teach better farming methods to the Montagnard farmers. Bill, from Oklahoma, will be working as hospital administrator and medical assistant in a clinic much like ours which is being built by the Vietnamese Protestant Church in Pleiku with the assistance from Vietnam Christian Service.

This clinic will serve primarily the Montagnard or tribal peoples of the area surrounding Pleiku. They are Vietnam's minority population. They live in the inland mountainous areas of the country which are about seventy percent of the area north of Saigon.

Each of the different tribes speaks its own language, all very different from Vietnamese. In appearance and culture, the Vietnamese people—the majority population of the country—resemble the Chinese. The Montagnards, however, resemble the Polynesian in appearance, and their culture and customs are reminiscent of the American Indians.

Pleiku is in the midst of Montagnard territory and I found it interesting for this reason among others. Nha Trang's surroundings are the typical palm tree studded rice paddies you see pictured in so much Vietnamese art. Pleiku, on the other hand, is surrounded by what looks like an over-sized, hilly, southern Ohio cow pasture.

Nha Trang is a fair sized, well-paved metropolis. Pleiku is a small town, criss-crossed only by about a dozen muddy roads. Nha Trang is a vacation and administrative area for the American military; Pleiku is a base for men who are fighting a war that is very near at hand. I was made acutely aware of this the first night when the mortar fire woke me.

The next day we visited a Vietnamese military hospital on whose surgical ward were several captured, wounded Viet Cong prisoners. We were able to talk to them a little. Their marked state of malnutrition made me wonder anew at the power of the political philosophy for which these men were willing to fight until apparently almost at the point of starvation and exhaustion. They looked as if they were barely out of their teens, shackled to their hospital beds with leg irons and constantly under armed guard.

Doc flew back to Nha Trang on Wednesday morning but I stayed in Pleiku until Friday morning when I flew to Saigon. I was delighted to meet the group of new Vietnam Christian Service workers who have arrived since I left Saigon. There are now forty-seven VNCS workers here and twelve more expected early in September. I spent about three days in Saigon visiting old friends, making new ones and visiting the new projects being started there. A medical project about eight kilometers out of Saigon and a community center and day care center project in the downtown area have been proposed, but any work of an administrative nature is infuriatingly slow due to insecurity and red tape.

Saigon has not changed much in the past three months except in increases in prices, traffic, confusion and Americans. So it was with little regret that I left for NhaTrang on Monday morning. As I sighted from the air the large white statue of the seated Buddha which overlooks this "pearl of the South China Sea," I had the unmistakable feeling of being glad I was "home."

September 11 marks the first elections this country has seen for many years. True, the elections are only for a National Assembly to choose a government and there will, no doubt, be difficulties and "unconstitutional" practices. The results will not be totally representative, but I have a vague feeling that it may be a step in the right direction for the solution of the myriad of internal political problems of South Vietnam. We expect increased Viet Cong terrorist activity between now and election day, especially in Saigon. Much of it will probably be directed against Vietnamese civilians and potential voters.

Nevertheless, I view the elections with faith and hope! We jokingly ask each other what we have packed for evacuation to Hong Kong on September 12 if elections go the wrong way, but none of us is really concerned at the prospect of elections.

I see now that you'll all have to read this epistle in installments to avoid eye strain. So I'd better stop while you can still see who is responsible for this long-winded travelogue! Thanks for letters from many of you. I wish I could answer them all. And many thanks for prayers in my behalf— be assured that you are remembered in mine!

7
At Election Day
And Holiday Time

Newsweek
September 19, 1966

Pregnant Choice

"Demons weep, God grieves, and anyone who goes out will vomit blood and die." Such was the fearful forecast that Viet Cong agents circulated throughout South Vietnam to discourage those who were inclined to go to the polls and vote in this week's Vietnamese election. And to make the message even plainer, squads of Viet Cong strong-arm men moved through the country's villages at night, knocking on doors, warning prospective voters against casting a ballot. Candidates were threatened with assassination; hints were dropped that polling places would be bombed.

As the day of the election approached, in fact, the Viet Cong did launch a series of scattered terror raids, making many people just a bit jumpy. Just how jumpy became clear when a plane zipping across the Saigon sky sent off a sharp sonic boom. At the sound, scores of nervous citizens hurled themselves into doorways for protection, newspaper cameramen rushed out into the streets to photograph the destruction they expected to find and Henry Cabot Lodge's car was halted by nervous U.S. Security guards, who promptly threw a cordon of bodies around the U.S. ambassador . . .

And yet, despite the campaign of intimidation, millions of Vietnamese were expected to go to the polls. To counteract the terror, the national police and the South Vietnamese military were on full alert. In the 5,238 polling places around the country, barricades were set up to prevent last-ditch terrorist attacks and ballot boxes were nailed down to prevent them from being snatched away. . . .

And the government of Air Vice Marshal Nguyen Cao Ky did its best to whip up election fervor. *Di Bau!* said government-printed signs plastered all over Saigon. It was the only election slogan that got any real attention. *Di Bau,* it seems, means "go vote." But it can also mean "get pregnant."

Of South Vietnam's 5,288,512 registered voters, the Ky government hoped that at least 60 per cent would heed the advice—in the political sense. In fact, the number of voters was made into a political test of strength between Ky and the Communists. Most of the voters, admitted Ky, might not know what they were voting for, but it was essential, he insisted, that they vote nonetheless . . .

August 28, 1966
NhaTrang

Dear Folks,

What a relief to be getting mail again. After more than two weeks with no letters, this past week I got two letters from you and heard from two of my sisters. All four letters were filled with encouragment which I didn't need quite as much the week after vacation as I had the week before.

This morning was children's day at the Vietnamese Protestant church we usually attend. It was much like at home. Three or four children's choirs sang, prizes were given for attendance, Bible study, and other activities. It was very interesting, even though I couldn't understand a word. That's not quite true; now and then I could pick up a word or two that was being said.

My dissatisfaction with my language progress (which, viewed objectively, isn't really too bad) is a symptom of my general dissatisfaction since I came here. Finally, just within the last few days I've begun to isolate what the trouble is. Just like when I was in nursing school and when I started working as a nurse, I feel so inadequate that I'm fighting to prove that I can do as well or better than anybody else at any and everything. I forget I can just sit back, relax and take it easy because just being me is really quite good enough. It's a lot of frustration and wasted effort to go around fighting the world but I do it so often when I'm unsure of myself. Maybe I can begin to relax now.

Well, it's a beautiful, warm, lazy Sunday afternoon. I work tonight but have the day free, so I am sitting here on the front lawn, feet propped on the fence enjoying the view of the sea. The sand flies, jellyfish, and work schedule have been so bad that I haven't been swimming for about three weeks! Isn't that a hardship?

The day is so lazy, in fact, that there really isn't much news to write about. A two-wheeled horse cart comes up the lane heavily loaded with visitors for the hospital; one of the staff goes by on his motor scooter; a few American soldiers, uniformed and armed but on free time, stroll down the beach; jets, prop planes, and helicopters are heard almost continuously. A typical quiet Sunday afternoon.

September 4, 1966
NhaTrang

Dear Folks,

The big news this week is that I've moved from the main staff house to a tiny house nearer to the clinic. We had to rent it since our staff is so large now. It is a Vietnamese-built house so, instead of the American "upper-class" style of living we've been accustomed to, Marcy and I are now living like lower middle-class Vietnamese. The house is simple (some of you might think "primitive," a more applicable adjective!) and looks something like the floor plan on the following page.

(Art never was my strong point but I think you can get an idea of what it's like.) It reminds me a lot of Aunt Grace's lake cottage, but a little more rustic. The bedrooms are constructed from concrete with a tin roof. The living room-dining room area is a tin roof over a very rough brick floor surrounded by screen walls. Only the front wall which faces the sea has large grass mats on pulleys which can be lowered to increase privacy and decrease the amount of rain coming through during the rainy season. We shall soon have the opportunity to find out how well it works for the rainy season is due to start about the first of October.

There is running water only in the sink at the back of the house. Therefore, practically all water must be carried from

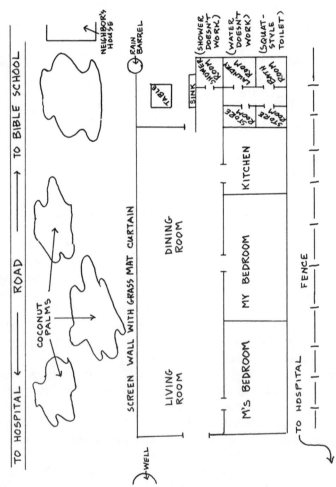

the well outside the front door. Over the well hangs a bucket attached to a rope and pulley. It looks romantic in pictures. I wonder if it is as romantic to actually have to use it! During rainy season, drawing water is not nearly so much work. There is a large rain barrel out on the back porch, under the end of the rain spout. No doubt that barrel will be full to running over during those several wet months.

I can't adequately describe Vietnamese toilets except to say that they are basically holes in the floor with a platform on each side. One straddles the hole, puts one foot on each platform and squats. The Vietnamese people squat-sit from the time they are children but it takes muscles which most Westerners, including me, haven't developed well!

We have electricity, but fixtures are few and far between and the current is temperamental and intermittent. So we also have candles. When I first saw the house, I thought it looked pretty grim, just as I've described it above. But now we have some furniture in, curtains at the bedroom windows, books on a bookshelf, glasses in the kitchen and towels on the clothesline, and it's home!

Last night was the first night we slept in it and it was then that I realized the greatest charm of this place: it's like camping out all the time! All those family vacations in a tent prepared me well. Now I find it quite natural to have to carry water and fall asleep looking out at the lights of the fishing boats on the sea and listening to crickets and frogs. My camera has arrived from Hong Kong to replace the one that was stolen, so I can soon send you pictures of our humble abode.

Well, it's past bedtime and tomorrow is Monday which means I must get up at 5:30 a.m. for language study.

September 11, 1966
NhaTrang

Dear Folks,

Well, election day in South Vietnam has come and gone without disrupting our peace and quiet too much. By that I mean we here at the clinic—American staff, Vietnamese staff and patients—are all still here and intact.

This week has not been without its share of excitement, however. Campaign posters and banners have been posted around town for nearly a month. This past week the parades began. Friday morning when Carl went to town, the main square of town was blocked off for such a parade already in progress. As he walked towards the square after parking the scooter, he heard a dull thud, saw a large puff of smoke and saw the people scatter; some explosive device had been set off in the crowd! Several people were injured but he does not think any one was killed.

I'm sure terrorist activity was common all over the country, although with such news coverage as we get no doubt you know better than we. Probably our little incident was not even reported in the news.

I didn't sleep too well Friday night. My roommate had gone to Hue to visit. I was alone in our little house here which is somewhat removed from civilization and protection. From twelve midnight until two a.m. it was like the Fourth of July around here except that it was spotter flares and gunfire at the bridges instead of firecrackers and Roman candles in the back yard! The dogs, of course, nearly went insane with every explosion, so it was not exactly conducive to slumber. Saturday night I slept in the staff house.

Over a week ago all American personnel around here received advice to stay off the streets and out of town; military personnel were put on "security condition: gray" which means "confined to base and quarters." This was strictly enforced for the military, and even early in the week when we went to town shopping, the streets were empty of Americans. Saturday evening when Carl and I went into town for a little while, we saw no other "round eyes" on the streets and the Vietnamese traffic was much decreased. Of course we drew more stares than usual but they were filled only with amazement and curiosity, I think, not hostility. Armed guards are everywhere, protecting the polling places and official buildings.

All day Saturday we were sending patients out on leave of absence to go home and vote and then come back to the hospital. This morning (Sunday) when I got to work, there was a large yellow and red striped, Republic of Vietnam flag-banner taped across the front porch pillars of the hospital. It was put up by one of the workers here at the hospital, I guess to say "We're in favor of the elections and we're voting."

There were several points about this election that seemed strange to me, reared in the tradition of American democracy. This election was for a national assembly, not a national leader. My information sources are not infallible either, but I hear that only sixty percent of the population in about twenty to twenty-five percent of the land area could vote. That is, only the people in the areas that are "secured" were allowed to go to the polls.

Their choice (here in NhaTrang, Khanh Hoa province area anyway) was one of two groups of three people each. Both are pro-government, anti-Communist and, I think, religiously homogenized (i.e., both Catholics and Buddhists). There is a sentence of life imprisonment to anyone caught trying to interfere with the elections. When people vote they receive a mark on their identification cards that they have done so. So, although voting is not exactly compulsory, any person without this mark will henceforth be subject to suspicion as a pro-Communist. Travel, movement, living and working will thus be restricted. No wonder so many of the patients asked permission to go home from the hospital on leave to vote.

After saying all of this, I think I'd be safer to send this out APO. In-coming mail is being held up again probably due to the elections. Heaven knows what out-going mail will be subject to.

I am including a picture of Dr. Harold and me working over a pathetic little baby who came in last week. He has severe malnutrition and the doctor was trying to start an IV in his leg vein. About two minutes after the picture was taken the baby stopped breathing. I gave mouth to mouth resuscitation until the doctor had finished the IV. The little one is still alive and doing a little better but is still very weak.

I had a "funny" experience last Tuesday night while going for a moonlight swim with several of the unit members.

I stood up under a jellyfish, not being able to see him in the dark. He must have been a big one, four to five inches in diameter, and he stayed on for about thirty to forty-five seconds before I could pry all the tentacles off. It felt like the bee and hornet stings I used to get when I was a little girl. We rubbed it with sand immediately to scrape off the jellyfish tissue. But, by the time I got back to the house, I had a swollen left arm with many white welts and a tortuous pattern of angry red lines on the inside of my left upper arm where the tentacles had been on the longest. I spent a restless night Tuesday looking for a comfortable position but the pain only lasted about two days. Now it just looks like a grotesque tattoo which is beginning to peel off. Needless to say I haven't been swimming since!

September 22, 1966
NhaTrang

Dear Folks,

This past weekend and the first of this week were really busy and I am only just now recuperating. Last Friday, the doctor and his wife and one of the nurses went over to Pleiku because Sunday was the dedication and opening of the new clinic which Vietnam Christian Service has helped to build there. It, too, is staffed by a Mennonite doctor from Pennsylvania and a Canadian Mennonite nurse—both friends of our staff here. As our Pax-man took our folks to the plane at the NhaTrang airport, a plane arrived from Saigon bringing a VNCS couple up for a weekend stay here. Shortly thereafter, another couple and their young son arrived from Quang Ngai for the weekend here and none of these people were expected in advance. Luckily we had a few empty beds!

Friday night my roommate and I did our first entertaining in our new house. We brought the guests over, sat around on our newly covered "floor cushions" and sang. Then we served popcorn and Vietnamese tea. That's real style, huh? That's about as fancy as we'll be able to get because our little hot plate takes about two hours to heat a small pan of water for tea!

Sunday, Marcy was the nurse on duty at the hospital and she was really busy with three babies with meningitis or encephalitis. One wasn't very sick, one died, and the other needed almost constant attention.

Emma, Carl, and I went up to the Bible School seminary—Thanh-Hoc-Vien Tin-Lanh—for the opening ceremonies for the new school term. It was a very impressive service with all the important ministers of the area present.

Sunday night I worked, and it was a long night. I slept from 2 to 4:30 a.m., but most of the rest of the night I sat on the baby's bed watching his respirations. When I dozed, I put my hand on his belly so that if he stopped breathing I'd feel it immediately and wake up. By morning he was doing a little better and Marcy relieved me in the hospital so I could go home and catch some sleep. Monday night I worked again and the baby was much better.

By that time, however, we had two other children in from the same village as the first baby and all with similar symptoms. Fortunately, these latter two were not quite so sick as the first. This is the same village from which, about two months ago, we had seven children at one time with the same symptoms.

And, as if the infection isn't enough to deal with, there are other complications. We had put a naso-gastric tube in one of those children in order to be able to feed it. It was simply too weak to eat. One afternoon, as I tried to give the child feeding fluid, the tube was plugged. Nothing would go in or come out. I tried in every way I knew how to get the tube unclogged: I tried flushing with water, twisting the tube, moving it in and out a little. Nothing worked; it was still plugged.

I had no choice but to pull it out and replace it with a new one. So I pulled it out and could scarcely believe my eyes when I saw what was plugging it up. Jammed into the small outlet hole in the end of the tube was the end of a *round worm,* almost as thick as the tube and two-thirds as long as the child! The worm was still alive and was writhing and wiggling as I pulled it out with the tube. No wonder the child was malnourished!

But, back to this week. Monday night I slept in the chair in the living room and only went over to the hospital four times during the night for a half hour to an hour at a time. But by Tuesday I was beat, so I took off two hours in the busiest part of the morning and came home and slept.

I'm finally pretty well caught up on sleep but I've done nothing else for a week, so I'm behind on correspondence. I'm also just about ready to put the sleeves in a dress I haven't worked on for a week. Our treadle sewing machine takes some getting used to but it works like a dream.

September 29, 1966
NhaTrang

Dear family,

Today is Trung Thu: the children's holiday of lights. It's a little bit like Halloween, but better, because on this night the children make or buy lanterns (at home we'd call them Japanese lanterns.) They then light candles inside the lanterns and, after it gets dark, they parade with their lanterns, play games and enjoy treats. The orphanage, of course, has a special celebration, so tonight we went over to observe the festivities.

As we approached the orphanage gate we saw the parade of lights approaching accompanied by the rhythmic beating of a barrel drum. We joined in the parade and then we saw the "dragon" which had three sets of boys' feet sticking out below his uneven back. The dragon led the parade, dancing along at the head of the column of lights, keeping time to the beating of the drum. Beside him danced his "keeper" who had a large papier-mâché head with a grinning, Chinese face.

The parade wound up and down the road a few times. Then we followed it back to the orphanage director's house. There the director had tied a small prize of money to a wire high above the dragon's head as a test of his jumping ability. Despite a high chair and the lights of twenty or thirty lanterns, the poor dragon had to go hungry as he couldn't reach the prize!

Then we went off to the auditorium where we all gathered to see the program that had been prepared by the children. Each dormitory unit, I think, prepares a little skit to present to their fellows and guests like us. Some of the skits had groups singing; the "dragon" danced again a few times, and there were various humorous skits including everything from beggars to pirates to doctors. Some of the little skits were really hilarious even though we couldn't understand too much of what was being said.

The auditorium was packed with orphans of all sizes and ages. There were also various people of the community in attendance, like ourselves and other hospital staff. After the program, the "dragon" led all the children off to the dining hall for a special treat of holiday sweets. It was a lovely evening.

This morning on my day off, I walked over to a nearby village to visit a friend of mine, one of my Vietnamese teachers during those early months of language study in Saigon. We were going to study Vietnamese, but I discovered that he had gotten a job and wasn't home. So I visited with his family instead. His father, I found out, had been ill with TB for six years and had been too sick even to come to clinic for the past six months.

I was shocked when I saw him. He looked so terribly weak and thin. After about half an hour of persuasion, he agreed to come to the clinic with me if I came for him in the car. After examining him, Doc said he has only about six inches of one lung left functioning and there is nothing we can do for him. He will probably only live a few weeks more but he chose to go back home to die. So we gave him medicine and I took him back home. We gave him a prescription for streptomycin and I took one of his sons into NhaTrang to buy the medicine.

By this time my friend was home from his work, so I told him of the situation. Naturally he was very sad and I was sad to have to break the news to him. I am glad, however, that there was something I could do for him and his family.

His father has been unable to work since he became ill, so my friend and his mother both work to make ends meet. They live in a house of wooden upright supports and walls made of flattened cardboard boxes. But all extra money is used to send the younger children to school.

Such experiences help me to get past all the differences and peculiarities of this country and begin to see it on the level of the individual person. I'm beginning to collect a few personal friends (even though I can't talk to them too well) and to see the patients as individuals and treat them as such.

We have a cancer patient just now who is dying. Most of last week she kept the entire ward in an uproar with her constant piteous crying and moaning, apparently from pain and fear. We thought that the kindest thing we could do was to keep her sedated and quiet. We were using large doses of sedation several times a day. This week our meager supply of sedative medication is almost exhausted. So, out of desperation, I've made it a special little project of mine to give her half an hour of my time about three times a day. I spend the time in cleaning her up, changing her bed and just sitting and talking with her or, most often, just sitting with her in silence.

At first she didn't know what I was doing. But for the past three days she has not needed any medication and she has been quiet and awake. She occasionally smiles at me now and, yesterday, asked me to pray with her before I left her. I told her "even God couldn't understand my Vietnamese." She replied, "He understands English, doesn't he?" So I prayed in English.

She's so much more at peace with herself now that I think she's ready to die. That's part of what I mean by being able to finally begin to see Vietnam on the level of the individual. This has been a happy and rewarding week! I'll bet you were afraid after all this time that you'd never ever hear me say that, weren't you?

The jellyfish sting is healing well and will leave only an ugly scar which, I hope, won't be too conspicuous. Last Sunday night, in the midst of a preview of the coming rainy season, I slipped on the wet front porch steps. I now have a plum-colored bruise the size of a large orange on my left buttock. I also suspect a bruised or slightly cracked tail bone. The bruise is not too sore anymore but there seems to be one spot on my "tail" on which I cannot sit!

As if I didn't have enough to do already, week after next I begin teaching English to a class which will possibly be as large as fifty. Me, who never taught anybody anything, trying to teach fifty adults something I don't understand too well myself! And I can't even talk to them very well! I can't help but laugh when I think about it. But, after spending about an hour and a half last night writing out lesson plans for the first five lessons, I'm rather eager to get started. How I wish I had some of you experienced teachers to give me a little expert advice! I'll let you know how it goes. If I'm lucky the whole deal will fall through!

We've been eating especially well the past few days. The "headmen" of a fishing village up the beach brought us a "thank you" gift for our care of several sick children from their village. We had saved five out of seven of the kids who had come in several weeks ago very seriously ill with some kind of infection we never really identified.

Their gift was proportionately generous: a huge tray (perhaps a yard in diameter) full of fresh seafood, still alive! There were lobsters crawling over shrimp and several other types of deep sea creatures. I thanked them profusely as they put it in my hands and tried to look properly grateful. But once I was out of their sight, I ran for the kitchen as fast as I could go and yelled for the cook to relieve me of that slimy burden! The seafood tastes delicious when cooked, and I definitely prefer the creatures dead and boiled!

October 6, 1966
NhaTrang

Dear Folks,

The rainy season is officially upon us. Last Tuesday it rained continuously from one a.m. until nine a.m. Probably because of this, we only had twenty patients in clinic. Then the sun came out steamy hot. That afternoon in fifteen minutes time a storm blew in off the sea which dashed rain under the closed front door of the staff house and halfway across the living room floor. Both bedrooms on the front of the house were drenched through closed shutters. Needless to say our little cottage here in the coconut grove was nearly washed off the map.

Yesterday it rained for about six to eight hours at various times, sometimes a downpour and sometimes a drizzle. Today it's already been raining for three hours and it's not noon yet. I can see how this season of the year could get depressing after two or three months of continuously gray skies.

I was having so much pain in my lower back last week when lifting and sitting that I finally had Dr. Harold examine it. He thinks the tailbone was probably broken when I fell down the front porch steps two weeks ago. Of course there's nothing that can be done about it but I'm doing a lot of standing up and lying down these days.

Last night was my first English class and the estimate of fifty students was about twenty too low! They range in age from seven to twenty-seven with varying levels of education and ability. The class is held at a Catholic school a kilometer west from the hospital. The students are mostly fishermen and their children from nearby villages. They are not well-to-do or well-educated people. There are a few soldiers but perhaps two-thirds of the class are children. I doubt that they'll learn much English with seventy students and one teacher but at least it will keep them off the streets!

Speaking of teaching: the plans for the proposed nurses' training school are coming along so well that we are now choosing what subjects we wish to teach and beginning to prepare lectures. Try not to laugh too hard when I tell you I will be teaching anatomy and physiology and microbiology. How I wish for some of those textbooks I left at home! The prospect of teaching sobers me, to be sure. But the idea of teaching nursing students these basic subjects in Vietnamese really has me scared.

On the other hand, I've had more formal training in these subjects than any of the other nurses here and the students coming in to the school will have had none at all. So, as I told Ruth, the nurse who is in charge of the school, "I'll try."

I'm excited at the prospect of teaching in a training school but the mundane task of preparing lectures is bogging me down right now. It takes so long. I have thirteen one or two hour lectures to prepare and get translated in the next few weeks so we can begin a training program with our present staff as soon as possible. And I thought I was busy before! Ha!

October 13, 1966
NhaTrang

Dear Sisters,

In an earlier letter, Mother asked if there was anything the church women's work group could take on as a project to help us out here. The most sensible and useful things would be linen goods of all sorts: sheets (60 by 108), pillowcases, small and large, both towels and washcloths, rolled muslin strips for bandages, pajama pants (we've got enough tops for now) and bright colored or figured squares of cloth eighteen inches square or larger, hemmed on all four sides. These we use for covers on the patients' bedside tables. Linen supplies of all sorts are always wearing out and disappearing, so we have a continuous need. The safest way to send such things is through one of our supportive church organizations. They can be packed in metal barrels and sent to us here via Saigon. They may not arrive for eight to ten months but they probably will arrive.

Doc is on vacation for a week and when he returns it will be time for Dr. Harold and Esther to go back to Saigon for language study. So we are reduced again to one doctor for the next two months. Business is booming as usual here. In fact, sitting as I am just now, in the midst of preparations for nursing classes to begin November 1, the booms are deafening! I feel a little swamped with work just now and Marcy has been sick for a week which increases work for the rest of us in the clinic, too. Oh, well, what doesn't get done doesn't get done.

Dr. and Mrs. I. W. Moomaw, former Brethren missionaries to India, are here for a short visit with us just now. They have been in Vietnam for about two or three months and next week they will head back to the States via India where they will visit for a few months. During their many years in India they wrote several books about the work there. *Crusade*

Against Hunger is one of those books. Their next book will be about Vietnam and they are here collecting background information for that book. They will be going back to Saigon this afternoon and I want to send these letters out with them to be mailed from there.

Tell the children to study hard in school. I'll bet I'd hardly recognize them by now! What would the family think if I decided to extend my stay into the fall of '67 or even longer?

October 29, 1966
NhaTrang

Dear Folks,

Yesterday I told our Saigon office that I would extend my term of service until the spring of 1968. I was waiting for a reply from some of you homefolks before making this decision final, but the office needed to know right away. I told them that this decision was still subject to a veto from family but, as always, I did not expect that veto to come.

I am still tired today from having spent nearly half the night two nights ago in thought and prayer about this matter. In all due respect and love to my family, the only good reason I could think of for coming home is that some day I hope to settle down to a home of my own. Hopefully that home would include husband and family but that looks pretty dismally distant from here. Still, as I told the folks at the Saigon office, if the Lord intends for me to have a husband, I'm sure one will be found no matter where I am.

The reasons for my staying are more complex. NhaTrang is a pleasant and exciting place to work. There's much work here that needs to be done and it is worthwhile work. I promised the church offices at home that I would stay if I could. Two years is the regular BVS contract for overseas service. Much money has been invested in me and one year is barely enough time to get started in the work and the language.

The nursing school may be getting underway before too long and I am eager to be able to help out in that. But most of all, I'm sure, is the challenge that is here and my own dissatisfaction in how I have been meeting it.

There is plenty of challenge here: in the work itself, language skills, culture adjustment, in unit living and, above all, the challenge to live as a Christian in this situation. I'm not happy yet (or even pleased) with my performance in any of these areas. So, of course I can't come home yet.

I think I have it within me to do better and an extension will give me more time to try to prove it to myself. Maybe that's not a very good motive but I know it's true. I think it is the right thing for me to do to stay longer. But suddenly tonight I am overwhelmed by a wave of homesickness and loneliness!

November 3, 1966
NhaTrang

Dear Folks,

Thank goodness for old stationery to use up so I can save a little money. I have lists and lists of shopping I want to do; but you know how tight I am about spending money even when I have it. When I don't have it, it's even harder for me to spend. Consequently, I've done very little shopping yet.

Tuesday of this week was a Vietnamese holiday. It was the anniversary of the fall of the Diem regime. So, in typical Vietnamese fashion, official offices were closed Monday, Tuesday, and Wednesday. Tuesday, there were parades and public entertainment in the town square in NhaTrang. But since we gave all of our Vietnamese staff the day off, we all had to work.

Mail piled up for three days, of course, and when we finally got it, I got the nicest collection of letters I've received in a long time. The ladies of the church wrote the "homefolksiest" letter at their work day. I was happy for it and I wish there were some way to reply. Please give them my sincere thanks at their next meeting.

It scares me a little to think that so many good people at home think I am doing such a "good work." If they could only see me on days when I'm relaxing on the beach and swimming all day I'm sure they would wonder about it. Or worse yet, they'd have real doubts if they could see me on days when I pass my frustration level by ten a.m. and by noon I'm difficult to everybody and by afternoon I'm impossible. Then I'm sure they'd question the use of mission money on somebody like me!

But, thank goodness there are other days, too. For example, there was a day of bathing, clothing, and feeding a little boy with mental illness who was manageable for the first time in a week. Another day on which we sent home a baby that had twice been given up for dead when it first came into the hospital. There are days of talking, joking, and visiting with my Vietnamese staff and friends in their language. These days help balance out the expenditure of church mission money!

Tomorrow afternoon is our first nurses' training class with the hospital staff. My doubts about my skill as a teacher and about the usefulness of the content of the course I have written are growing by the hour. Of course, they can only be answered by going ahead with it.

Well, one more letter to answer. But a sunny day in rainy season is too good to waste sitting inside at a typewriter. I must spend part of it down on the beach!

November 17, 1966
NhaTrang

Dear Folks,

Extending my term of service here has created a few minor problems. My wardrobe was definitely collected for only one year. I have, however, managed to make three dresses since I came and I think that I will have enough for church, shopping, going out to dinner, and traveling. Most of my off duty time at home I spend in *quan* (the loose fitting pajama-type Vietnamese trousers) and a loose blouse. The other American women on this project (all Mennonites) do not wear trousers, so I have yet to wear my blue jeans. The *quan,* however, don't seem to be quite as objectionable to them, and that loose outfit is very comfortable. The *quan* also keep the flies and bugs off the constant sores on my legs. So I am getting another pair made and cutting off a dress to make another blouse to go with them.

There's no use trying to send any of my clothes from home because I've lost so much weight. I'm down to 112 pounds now despite the fact that I am eating very well.

As to my working wardrobe, I'm nearly in rags and barefoot. Most of the time I wear sandals to work. Those I

can easily buy here because my narrow feet fit easily into Vietnamese shoe sizes. It's the rest of me that is too big for the culture, and uniforms are a real problem. Two of my four are in
rags. I rescued one out of a missionary barrel which the clinic
received and I hemmed it up. It may be wearable and I may be
able to buy one more from one of the other nurses here. But
two will hardly be enough for another year!

Staying on another year will also give me a chance to do
some of the shopping I haven't had time for. I went this morning and enjoyed myself so much. I saw so many things which
you or I would enjoy that I will probably go again. I don't plan to
buy anything big or expensive on my $30 a month, but I do
want to buy some things which will serve to remind me of this
experience. I think I will look for a tea service of Vietnamese
"crockery." It isn't especially beautiful, as china goes, but the
blue dragon pattern is so typical that it will always remind me
of Vietnam and our patients when I use it.

The present count stands at sixteen for Christmas at
NhaTrang. At least you won't have to worry about my getting
lonely! I may take a week of vacation about that time, too. Of
course we'll be homesick, but we won't be alone.

Classes are going well, both the English language
instruction down at BaLang and the anatomy and physiology
classes with our hospital staff. On Sunday one of my English
classes is going for a picnic at a nearby scenic spot and I'm
going along.

Since I made the decision to stay, most days have confirmed it to be the right decision. But, as in any foreign service,
it is not the natives that are the biggest problem in adjustment. I've told you before of some of the problems existing in
unit life here, mostly resulting from incompatible per-
sonalities. I, personally, am very grateful for the solitude which
our new living arrangement provides. Before the unit rented
our little cottage in the coconut grove, we nurses were all
sharing bedrooms. That was difficult at best and at times
almost intolerable.

Just this week some of these personality problems have
more or less come to a head with Marcy ready to request
transfer because of difficulty working under Doc's permissive

style of administration. Everyone's a bit on edge and I don't know what the outcome of it all will be. What we need right now are a pair of mature, objective houseparents. The VNCS personnel director and his wife are spending Thanksgiving with us, so perhaps that will be a good time to talk this out. The sweetness and love of the living situation here has not noticeably improved since I arrived either. So I will be willing to transfer, too, if it would be for the good of all. However, I'm sure we'll weather this somehow. This, too, shall pass.

Well, it's almost suppertime and we're having company tonight. I'd better be on time.

November 17, 1966
NhaTrang

Dear Sisters,

Mother will no doubt tell you, but I'll also tell you myself: I have extended my term for an additional year. The only condition to this decision is that my family approves. I wrote in more detail to the folks a week ago. You can read their letter for my reasons for staying. I am going to be a little short on clothes for another year, but if I don't encounter any problems more serious than that I will be fortunate.

Today's been a lazy day. Thursday is regularly my day off and last week I spent it on the beach all day. Today I went to town for the entire day. I went shopping, ate lunch out and, this afternoon, went to visit a missionary family in NhaTrang who have a piano. Oh, what a wonderful feeling to play again. I lost track of time and got back home late.

All of my classes are going well and I am enjoying them very much. I am teaching anatomy and physiology to our hospital staff in the trial run of our nurses' training course. I am also teaching English to about fifty children and adults in BaLang, a little fishing village down the beach from the hospital. The English classes are one night a week. I'm not sure anybody else is learning anything but I am, and I'm having fun doing it.

On Sunday, the students in my second English class, another Vietnamese teacher and I are all going on a picnic on the rocks near the hospital. The students are doing pretty well but I think I'm learning almost as much Vietnamese from them as they are learning English from me!

I'm thinking already how much I'm going to miss the family at Thanksgiving and Christmas this year. But it looks like we're going to have a good celebration of our own. At latest count there are about a dozen or more other people planning to spend Christmas here with us, so we won't be lonely. But we'll be thinking about home, that's for sure!

November 25, 1966
NhaTrang

Dear Folks,

I hope that by this time you've received the latest edition of the newsletter. I'd hate to have to write it over because it got lost in the mail. If you haven't gotten that letter yet you also haven't received my statement of why I extended my term a year. So for two reasons I hope the letter didn't get lost in the mail.

Unfinished work is beginning to get me down all of a sudden. My correspondence is falling behind again; I have another series of six lectures to write; a little sewing and mending to do; it's been ages since I've studied language and there's so much reading I want to do. But in the past three weeks I don't think there have been more than four or five days when we didn't have company for a meal or overnight. And, of course, they needed to be entertained.

Last night for Thanksgiving dinner there were fourteen of us; that is, our unit and eight guests. That knocks a hole in plans to get work done, but we really had an enjoyable time. What a feast we had to add to the good company: turkey, potatoes and gravy, as well as a tin of cranberry sauce left over from last Christmas. Afterwards we went to a special English language church service for servicemen and missionaries in NhaTrang.

December 1, 1966
NhaTrang

Dear Folks,

Can you believe that it's December first already? I find it a little hard to comprehend. It has been cooler lately; maybe even as cold as the fifties. The rains continue about half the time and, except for the green grass and palm trees, it looks gray, dismal, and wintry outside. The sea is absolutely gorgeous this time of year as the rains and storms whip it up to a boiling cauldron of waves and breakers. But, before I wax too poetic, I'd better get on with the business at hand.

Yes, I sent the Christmas edition of the newsletter about the first of November. I sent it just before we got APO privileges, so it went out Vietnamese mail. It panics me a little to think that it may be lost. I do not have a copy of the contents and it takes me about two or three days to compose one of those masterpieces. All I remember of the contents was this: a discussion of rainy season, our new little house, the national elections, and I said almost the same things I had told you in a previous letter.

That was about all except that, as you know, I can get pretty long-winded on each and every topic! The closing paragraph went something like this: "Christmas is fast approaching and many of you will also be spending it away from home for the first time. Some of us will be spending it farther away from home than ever before but the message of Christmas knows no boundaries. The angels' song of "Peace on earth and goodwill among men" seems pretty faint here. But Christmas means God's love being born on earth and a little bit of Christmas is happening all over again in every crib in United States or the corner of every Vietnamese household where a baby cries and a mother loves. My prayers will be with you in this season of joy."

Why don't you just take the portions out of my previous letters to you on the subjects I mentioned. Edit them, tack this paragraph on the end, and send it out if the other letter doesn't come in time? I don't know when I'll find the time to write it all over again. Just now I have another monthly hospital report due, a report due to our Saigon office, arrangements to make for taking a week of vacation after Christmas, and preparations for a Christmas party for the hospital staff.

Your idea about sending to me the copies of *American Journal of Nursing* which are accumulating at home is excellent if it wouldn't be too expensive. I could use them for pictures and reference material for class then I could leave them here when I come home. I certainly will not need them at home as I can always go to a reference library to have access to back issues.

Periodical reading material sometimes gets in very short supply here so perhaps I would have time to read some of the old issues I have not yet digested. Then, too, I'm a little home-sick for renewed acquaintance with high quality, American hospital type nursing again.

I think I forgot to tell you about the picnic that my English class and I went on about two weeks ago. Since I didn't trust myself to drive with so many people in the car, Doc drove over to the school at BaLang to pick up the students. We each brought lunch for ourselves and spent the day on the rocks and the beach near the hospital.

It is one of the beauty spots of this entire country. The national government recently bought some of the land in order to make a national park or monument of the area of the rocks. The rocks look like so many marbles poured out by a giant's hand. And right out at the point that juts into the sea, there are two columns consisting of one rock balanced on another.

The area is called Hon Chong, that is, husband rock. The students told me in "Viet-ninglish" that the larger of these two rock columns is the husband, the smaller is the wife. The hus-band went away to war and was gone for many years. Some-one reported to the wife that he had been killed. After waiting for him some time longer, she went out to the seaside and killed herself in her grief. The husband came home, found her dead, then killed himself so that he could be near her.

We had a lovely picnic. Then the rain drove us to seek refuge in our little house off the beach. There we sat around looking at pictures in magazines from America and Canada and at photographs. We sang songs of Vietnam, Korea, United States, and China. The students are still talking about the picnic. They talk of it so often that now the other English class is clamoring to go on one. I think we will take them next week or the week after.

We had a wonderful Thanksgiving. The personnel director from VNCS Saigon office, Sam Hope, and his wife and three boys, ages seven, nine, and ten, spent about four days with us over the holidays. Also three members of the VNCS unit at Quang Ngai got stranded in NhaTrang with no flights out to Quang Ngai for three days, so they shared our turkey, too.

Well, I must write to the church offices and find out about vacation policies. My contract for service is in the package of books which was mailed by boat mail and hasn't arrived yet. I've written them twice before with other questions and have yet to get an answer. Perhaps, if I give them our APO address this time, the third time will be the charm!

Oh, one more thing I must tell you. The priest at the school where I teach English gave me two kittens in exchange for one of our dog's pups. The kittens are really cute but I will be glad when they learn not to use my underwear shelf for their bathroom! I'm hoping that they'll learn to catch lots of mice when they grow up to justify all the care and feeding of them now. The hospital is almost overrun with rats and mice and I thought the cats might help. Right now they're smaller than the mice! I've no doubt the rest of our pups will end up flavoring *pho* (soup) for some of our patients.

December 15, 1966
NhaTrang

Dear Folks,

Only ten days left until Christmas and I have yet to really catch the spirit. Christmas carols and rain-dripping palm trees just don't seem to go together. Your packages all arrived last weekend delivered to me by someone who came up from Saigon. Sis's package also arrived. She had sent it APO and our Paxman who picked up the mail got royally "cussed out" for it. He passed that message on to me but I was still happy for the package!

Now we have several brightly-wrapped packages under our artificial Christmas tree. We're going to be kept too busy this season to get homesick, I think. Yesterday afternoon was the dedication of our new TB hospital building which was just completed. Saturday night is the Christmas program at the NhaTrang Tin-Lanh Church, and the clinic staff sings. We also sing next week at the Vinh Phuoc Church. The Bible School and orphanage each have a Christmas program, too.

I've received Christmas cards from so many good people and I've appreciated them all so much. I wish I could thank each person individually. What did you ever do about my Christmas newsletter? I shall be eagerly awaiting my copy of my letter to see what I wrote!

I shall miss you all at Christmas.

May you have a
blessed Christmas
and a
joyous New Year.

Cầu cho Ông có
một Lễ Giáng-sanh
phước-hạnh
và một năm mới
vui-tươi.

P.S. The dedication of the new TB hospital building yesterday deserves more than just a brief mention. It was attended by a rather impressive assemblage of dignitaries for our humble establishment. Most of the dignitaries were missionaries of the NhaTrang area, the pastors of the Tin-Lanh churches in NhaTrang and Vinh Phuoc, most of the faculty of the Bible School, the director of the orphanage, an American military chaplain whose unit had donated help to build the place, two Korean chaplains from a nearby Korean military camp, the director of the division of health of Khanh Hoa province, two Franciscan monks (French Vietnamese) from the nearby leprosarium which they operate. Then there were, of course, the hospital patients, staff, friends, and hangers-on who came out of curiosity. And, most remarkable of all, for two and a half hours it didn't rain! Music was provided by the hospital staff, a choir of orphans from the orphanage next door, and some missionaries. The president of the hospital board and Doc each gave a short speech and there was a ribbon cutting ceremony. All very impressive and nice!

December 29, 1966
NhaTrang

Dear Folks,
    Perhaps you'd like a word of explanation about the note enclosed with this letter. The young G.I. who wrote it dropped in here about three days ago. On his way back to his base camp up near Tuy Hoa from his R and R leave, he found himself stranded in NhaTrang for several days. Looking around the countryside, he found us.
    He's an average young GI: he doesn't know what he's doing here in Vietnam, wishes he were any place but Vietnam, homesick and scared silly every time he goes out on a mission which is quite often. He is thoroughly antagonistic to Vietnam, the culture and the people, probably because all of his experiences have been with Vietnamese it is hard to like. I'm sure this is the main reason Carl invited him out to stay for a few days. He's enjoying his stay; even seems to be enjoying our Vietnamese staff and friends. He agreed to write a letter to you for me today while I ran errands.

All Christmas packages arrived in good time and good shape. Thanks loads to everybody.

The birthday of the Prince of Peace has come and gone again. In this place, at this time, it's hard to see the effects of his coming. But then, I guess in order to be real, it must be felt, not seen.

Newsweek
January 2, 1967

Strange Interlude: Peace on Earth

Even in the gray treadmill war in Vietnam, it was a season for hope against hope—the season when, only a year ago, the U.S. grounded its bombers for 37 days and put on one of the gaudiest peace offensives in diplomatic history. And so, U.S. troops mounted a lonely and wary watch over another Christmas truce last weekend, hope sprang again, only modestly dimmed by the disappointment of the past. If the fighting could be turned off for 48 hours over Christmas and 24 more over New Years's—so the persistent question ran around the world—why not simply stop it entirely and get the struggle at long last to the conference table?

. . . And so the fighting went on down to the moment when, on the morning before Christmas, the guns were to fall silent. In Vietnam, for those who were lucky, Christmas was turkey or duck for dinner, Bob Hope, Cardinal Spellman, or Billy Graham for dessert; for those who were not, it was C-rations and chlorinated water under a stuffy squad tent 8,000 miles from home. The hopes that made the stateside headlines meant at best, in the foxholes, that death might take a 48-hour holiday—and, even then, few GIs had forgotten the 84 Viet Cong-initiated incidents during the 1965 Christmas break. Nor was it lost on anyone that, on the very day Arthur Goldberg delivered his letter to U Thant, the first elements of yet another U.S. division were landing south of Saigon.

Peacemakers
May 2, 1967

". . . Blessed are the peacemakers for they shall be called the children of God . . . "
Peacemakers . . . peacemakers . . . Vietnam's number one need. God, just who are the peacemakers anyway?

Not just here in Vietnam but everywhere in the world:
 who are really the peacemakers?
Are they the protest marchers with their specific but idealistic
 "answers"? Are they the soldiers who risk their necks in the
 line of duty to secure peace (or at least pacification) for a
 few more people for a few more days?
Are they the legislators who hold the power to negotiate
 peace but who also establish unreasonable conditions
 necessary for negotiations to begin?
Or are they, perhaps, that vast number of people, confused
  and discouraged by the Vietnamania of press and
  public expression
who simply retreat from consideration of the conflict?
God, who really are the peacemakers;
 those worthy to be called your children?
 And where are they now,
 when and where they're needed so much?
"They're here, at work all over in my world.
 You just mentioned some of the things that they are doing
  and there are many ways to make peace.
 For example, you: what did you do today?"
Oh, no, God. Not me.
I didn't do any peacemaking today.
In fact, I didn't do much of anything today.
Let's see . . . I just sat with a premature baby for awhile
 encouraging it to breathe:
  gave an old lady some "headache medicine";
  bandaged a thumb where a skin graft covered the piece
   blown out by a grenade.
And what else?
  I helped the doctor remove stitches from an eye now
   minus its cataract.
 I emptied urine bottles and
  spent many frustrating minutes trying to understand
   and be understood
 on nearly every subject from abdominal pain to how to
  record temperatures on charts.
No, God, I didn't get much peacemaking done today.

8

On Vacation

Newsweek
July 18, 1966

Where The Girls Are

From the sodden rice fields of the MeKong Delta and the bloody jungles of Tay Ninh and Zone D in South Vietnam, it is—astonishingly enough—just a matter of hours by air to the glittering shops of Hong Kong, the massage parlors of Bangkok and the striptease palaces of Tokyo. To be sure, the trip drags slowly for many of the two thousand or more GI's who fly out of Saigon each week bound for Rest and Recuperation (R&R) in these and other cities of the Orient. But before long, the chartered Pan American or MAC planes touch down, the deeply bronzed GI's pile out and disappear for a holiday that—for some at least—will help to rub out some of the ugliness and horror of the war.

In town, on their five-to seven-day leaves, the GI's must change into civilian clothes "to make themselves less conspicuous," but whether the R&R city is Tokyo, Hong Kong, Bangkok, Manila, Singapore—or even less predatory fleshpots like Penang or Kuala Lumpur—every tout, shopkeeper, and hooker in town can spot them from 50 yards. The GI's get taken often enough, to be sure, but most don't seem to care, and in the process they are leaving behind as much as $60 million a year in the more questionable coffers of the Far East . . . . .

There is little doubt about the main objectives of an R&R holiday. Instead of R&R, some of the soldiers call it L&L (for Liquor and Love)—and the description is reasonably accurate. In the Taiwanese capital of Taipei, for instance, bars like the American, the

Ebony and the Playboy cater to visiting GI's, while just 25 minutes away was the resort city of Peitou. There, the Americans have discovered, a call to a hotel clerk can bring a pretty young girl riding up on a Suzuki motorbike in ten or fifteen minutes. In Tokyo, some of the GI's head for the Showboat or the Albion Bar, where the waitresses in low-cut costumes wiggle their hips as they serve beer and whisky and can be persuaded—for an extra fee to accompany the GI to a nearby hotel. "The hotel I stayed in," explains a blue-eyed GI, "doesn't allow girls in rooms, but I managed to sneak one in. You know most of these girls in bars, the hostesses, you'd think they were prostitutes, but they really aren't. They're working for their families, helping to support a brother through college." . . . .

It is, of course, obvious enough why the GI's are so well liked in Hong Kong. When they enter a tailor shop the price automatically goes up. Bars charge them as much as $1.75 for a Coke, and the beautiful Chinese girls in their sexy, slit-thigh *cheong sams* know well how to handle the crew-cut Americans. Money evaporates and only a few are as far-sighted as the three marines who each recently plunked $100 down at the Cherry Bar and told the mama-san to make it last four days. The astonished lady actually did.

The fact is that most of the service-men on the R&R circuit, whether it be Hong Kong or anywhere else, are fully aware that many of the local people are after one thing—their money. But the GI's take it all with a smile. "Spending money is what I'm here for," said a 20-year-old marine in Hong Kong recently before flying back to Chu Lai. "Some of the people think we're too dumb to know we're being had. Fact is, we just don't give a damn . . ." How do you feel, though, when you've blown a bundle on a girl and a hangover? The answer came quickly. "What the hell," said the young marine. "Charlie [the Viet Cong] might get me tomorrow."

January 1, 1967
Hue

Dear Family,
        Since I have the use of a typewriter and carbon paper and for once have plenty of time, there's no excuse for me not writing to all of you at once for a change. However, there's one problem. I'm writing to you from Hue where I am vacationing. It is rainy season here, too, but here in rainy season, it is *cold!* Unfortunately, I packed so lightly for this ten day vacation that

both of my sweaters, my socks and heavy shoes, and long pants are back in NhaTrang. So I pad about the house in a sweater borrowed from Ken and socks borrowed from Paul, both of whom are much larger than I!

It's even worse, however, when I have to go outside. I have nothing to wear on my feet but rubber thongs. The puddles are ankle deep and the mud omnipresent. A half hour spent taking friends to the airport this morning means that both hands and feet are currently stiff with cold. And the boys of the unit can't build a fire in the fireplace until they take the stereo speakers out of it!

But perhaps you'd like for me to begin at the beginning and tell you about our Christmas. We had a wonderful time.

Starting more than a week before Christmas we began fulfilling our obligations for singing at special Christmas church services. We're not terribly good singers and when we eight Americans and Canadians sing by ourselves we always have to sing in English.

But, in Tin-Lanh circles around NhaTrang at Christmas, there is competition by everyone planning a program to see who can get the most missionaries to participate. So, of course, the *bac-si* (doctor) and *cac y-si* (all the nurses) have to sing.

So sing we did: the Saturday night before Christmas Eve, the Sunday before Christmas, Wednesday, and Saturday of Christmas week and twice on Christmas Day. It was fun because several of these times the whole staff of the hospital, Vietnamese and American, sang together and we sang in Vietnamese. Nearly all of the familiar Christmas carols have been translated, plus a few I never heard of. So it sounded almost like home when the staff would start singing carols off the back of the truck as we were on our way going somewhere to church.

From what I have been able to learn from others and observe for myself, Christmas in Vietnam for both Catholics and Protestants is centered in the church rather than in the home as is our American custom. The week before Christmas is filled completely with special programs and services in each of the churches of the area and, in our case, by each of the church-related institutions, also. There is usually a decorated Christmas tree, many colored lights all over the church, much singing of Christmas songs both by the congregation and by special groups. Special masses are said in the Catholic churches. In Protestant churches the special Christmas services include the reading of the Christmas story, special plays and pageants, and many lengthy prayers.

The hospital program was the first of the area this year on Wednesday night. It was quite well attended by staff, patients, the hospital board, and many friends of the community. Half of the staff spent the entire day decorating the back clinic porch with both pine and palm boughs, lights, and stars of colored paper. It was really lovely.

After the program, we Americans had invited the Vietnamese hospital staff to come to the doctor's house for a Christmas party. Before they came, we all passed out candy and cookies and some small gifts to the patients in the hospital. During this time, two of our dogs got into the house and ate up half of the pastries for the staff party. Was I angry! I have no idea if the dogs also licked the remaining pastries but there were enough left to serve our guests so we tried not to think of that possibility and we served them anyway! Almost the whole staff came. For awhile we played games such as pin the star on the Christmas tree. Carl showed some of the slides he has taken of the hospital during the past two years. Refreshments (what was left of them) were then served and we gave gifts to each staff member. I think they all had a good time. I know we did.

Thursday night was the Bible School program but I stayed home and nursed a cold I can't seem to get rid of. With my luck, in this cold weather it will turn into pneumonia!

Friday night was the orphanage program to which I very much wanted to go. However we "missionaries" were invited to the Christian Servicemen's Center for a buffet dinner meeting with Evangelist Billy Graham. It was interesting, especially the music, but I was sorry to miss the orphan's program.

Saturday night was the Christmas program at the nearby church. The church was beautifully decorated with dim lighting and a floor-to-roof Christmas tree decorated with colored lights. In the front of the church was a large globe rotating on its axis illuminated by light from a cross above it. One part of the program was the short play *The Visited Planet,* presented in Vietnamese, of course. It is the conversation between angels and the earth concerning God's special gift to the world. It was a wonderful program.

Naturally, with the church so beautifully decorated and with so many foreigners, both American and Korean, going in and out, the Buddhist kids of the neighborhood didn't want to be left out either. So they came by the score, carrying their little brothers and sisters with them on their hips. The seats of the church were filled to overflowing early. So the little visitors packed in around the edges and overflowed down the aisles.

Some of us who came in a little late did manage to secure an inch on a bench in the back amidst this curious crowd. We were finally driven to our feet because of the smell at head level (which is about child armpit level). It's rainy season, you see, and much too cold for swimming or bathing!

The children had such a good time. They had no idea of the customary behavior of a Protestant church service so they talked, laughed, and walked about at any and all times. But, like some people I've seen in churches back home, most of them left when the singing was over and the minister started to preach!

As I said before, Christmas in Vietnam seems to be a church holiday rather than a family holiday. The minister of the church I mentioned above must know that for many Americans, Christmas means family. Perhaps he suspected that those of us away from family could get a little homesick, especially on Christmas Eve. So he invited our clinic staff, an American military chaplain and his assistant, and a Korean chaplain and his assistant to his home. We are the only foreigners in the area without families. The pastor, his wife and the young people of the church served all of us a sumptuous "tea" consisting of about four or five courses. We had a lovely time and, of course, had no time to get homesick.

We got home just a little before midnight. Then we set about opening the Christmas presents which we had received from home. I will appreciate the new pair of pajamas but right now I wish they had been flannel or insulated with asbestos. Our housemaid likes the slippers you sent so much, Mother, that I wonder if you could make her a pair. The children's gifts are also being put to good use. I enjoyed one of the books while I was in bed with a cold and brought some of the others along with me when I came on vacation. The whole household at NhaTrang enjoyed the *More Grape, Pickle and Elephant Jokes* book.

Anyway, it was about 12:30 a.m. when the gifts had all been opened and we set out Christmas caroling. We sang for our Vietnamese staff, the faculty of the Bible School, and our American missionary neighbors. The Vietnamese just wrote us off as crazy Americans for tromping around at midnight waking people up with Christmas carols, I think. But the Americans appreciated it.

Christmas Day, I worked all day, but the staff sang at the Korean hospital at the base nearby. Then they came and passed out Christmas bundles to all of our hospital patients and the TB patients. That night we all sang at the church in NhaTrang. It, too, was beautifully decorated with palm branch wreaths on every pillar framing a lighted candle. About halfway through the service one of the wreaths caught on fire from the candle. One of our quick-witted nurses grabbed her Bible and beat it out so quickly that the people in front didn't even notice!

Somewhere in our Christmas caroling sojourns on Saturday night, Emma got bitten by a snake, type unknown. A flying trip to the Army hospital on Christmas Day for anti-venom serum made her feel better but her foot was very pain-ful and swollen. I delayed my planned New Year's vacation until she could at least walk. She still isn't back to work full time but I was advised by the rest of the staff to go ahead with my plans.

So, late Friday morning, Carl took me in to the USAID airport to get the courier flight north to Danang. I dislike travel in this country for several reasons: the uncertainly of travel arrangements, changeable weather conditions, occasional ground fire, and engine failure.

Doc had warned me all about the unpleasant things that could happen to me between NhaTrang and Hue, such as being stuck in Danang for four days waiting for a flight out to Hue; getting stranded at the airport out of the city with no way in or out; not having the correct street address of the people I was going to visit. He had experienced them all! However, he forgot one basic fact which is of great help when traveling in Vietnam: I am a woman.

Instead of the courier flight, I got on the Embassy special. I was the only passenger aboard and so I was ceremoniously seated in the co-pilot's seat in the cockpit. I was royally entertained during the entire trip by a personalized account of the flight plan and commentary about the scenery over which we were flying. The pilot was almost too solicitous with his offer of dinner together in a fancy restaurant in Saigon when I arrived. His interest cooled a little, however, when his proffered cigarette and drink were refused as I replied that I did not smoke or drink. He gave it one last try: "And I'll bet you don't . . . oh, never mind." So much for a fancy dinner in Saigon! Virtue is it's own reward, I guess!

We flew directly to Hue where an Embassy car met the plane and delivered me to the door of the VNCS office here in Hue. So for the past three days I have been visiting with the folks here, looking over their farm project, shopping at the Hue market, and getting drenched. It has been raining steadily ever since I came.

There are seven VNCS personnel here in Hue: a couple and five fellows. The fellows all live together in a separate house and it is the typical bachelor apartment: only it is five times worse because there are five of them! I find it is rather fun to cook and bake things for them because they like to eat so well.

I'm nearly out of paper. I'll try to write more from Saigon before I go back home. When I get back to work I'll not have time to write anymore.

P.S. Attending a New Year's Eve party here in Hue last night with the VNCS fellows was quite an experience, from the ridiculous to the poignant. There were, of course, lots of military men there, American and Australian, and only one or two other women, both Vietnamese. Early in the evening, two "mildly drunk" Aussies tried for nearly an hour to figure out what nationality I was. They didn't think I was French and, "You can't be American because Americans can't speak English as well as you do." They finally concluded I must be Australian!

Later in the evening, a "moderately drunk" American Green Beret broke down and cried like a baby as he told me what his last six months in the jungles had been like. He had watched as ten of his buddies in a fifteen man search team were blown up and gunned down around him. He had killed and burned but could not get these pictures out of his mind nor the blood off his conscience. He's headed for a pine box or a psychiatric discharge if he doesn't get out of here soon!

January 7, 1967
Saigon

Dear Folks,

Saigon is the same as always: big, noisy, dirty, crowded, expensive and—the only good thing—warm. After six days in Hue suffering from nearly frostbitten feet, I thought I'd never enjoy a cold shower again. But in the Saigon heat it feels good. There is one other nice thing about Saigon. That is meeting old friends again and making new friends of the people now arriving in the country to begin their work with VNCS.

After two days of tramping around the city I have gotten some shopping done. I bought a new pair of glasses frames for less than $6.00 and now I can see again. Gifts were purchased for everybody at NhaTrang and a futile fifteen block walk looking for crutches to buy for the hospital finished off the morning, and me! I dislike shopping anywhere but especially here. Yet, it has to be done.

You know I've always had trouble spending money because I'm such a tightwad. Well, here it's even more complicated. For example, stateside friends sent me a little money with their Christmas card with instructions to spend it on me. I can't think of anything I need. Another friend sent some money to be used to help the Vietnamese people in some special projects which we don't have money for. Well, every time I think of a good project—milk and/or vitamin drink in quantities for the hospital, crutches for the hospital, blankets—somebody gives it to us free and I can't get rid of the money! How's that for a switch?

Sunday, January 8
Saigon

I left a lot of work for myself to do over vacation. Now vacation is almost over and the letters aren't written and the tests aren't graded. Oh well, there's always tomorrow.

Please send copies of my newsletter to our Saigon office. They say they can take the place of my monthly reports!

January 12, 1967
NhaTrang

Dear Friends,

December here at Chan-Y-Vien Tin-Lanh, NhaTrang was filled with Christmas. The hospital continued caring for inpatients; the clinic daily treated all who came and every week saw surgery in progress as usual. But all of this, and even the august assembly of dignitaries for the dedication of the new TB hospital, were eclipsed for me by Christmas.

It started early with our first practices of Christmas carols, *tieng Viet* (in Vietnamese), to be sung at special community programs. The excitement continued throughout the month until the Christmas tree finally found its way back into the box and all the gifts were put away. It was filled with many special events I shall remember for a long time:

—the clinic porch, decorated with palm, pine, and colored lights, jammed with people and ringing with the strains of "Joy to the World" in Vietnamese

—a young TB patient hearing these same strains in the midst of a massive hemorrhage

—the Christmas greetings and gifts from our clinic staff, my English students, and other Vietnamese friends

—the dogs eating up half of the pastries for our staff party

—the seasonal greetings of a shop-keeper I hardly know and her refusal to take my money for the cards I had selected. "I know who you are," she smiled. "I've been to your clinic and you gave me medicine and I'm better now. I give you the cards."

—the holiday season drafting of a young Vietnamese friend, leaving his mother, widowed by the VietMinh, to fend for herself

—Christmas caroling at 1 a.m.

—passing out gifts to the patients

—the beautifully lit church on Christmas Eve filled to overflowing with worshipers and curious Buddhist children from the neighborhood. Closely packed together in a crowd around some of us who were seated, they gave off such an aroma as might have greeted the nostrils of the newborn Baby Jesus. But I don't think the Christ Child minded 2000 years ago and I'm sure the perfume on Christmas Eve, 1966 didn't give offense, either. The children enjoyed themselves thoroughly, often to the distraction of the rest of us.

Yes, December was filled with Christmas and there was no room for homesickness. I thought of you all as the season approached and I sometimes wondered how the holidays were being spent in the States this year. But I had no envy of the "Christmas gifting rush" I remembered from previous years. This year I was caught up in a different kind of rush.

Vietnamese Christmas seems to center in the church and not the home as is the habit in the States. That may be true because so many homes and families are no longer intact. In the absence of blood relatives, people turn to their spiritual family. So every church organization and/or institution has a Christmas program. Not only did we have a program for the patients and community but we and the Vietnamese staff of the clinic were invited to sing at most of the other programs. So, the resulting rush of rehearsals, parties, and programs kept our schedule busy for weeks.

It was a truly joyous season marred only by the snake bite sustained by one of our nurses during our Christmas Eve midnight caroling. Luckily for all, it was only a mildly poisonous ground snake and, with the help of some Army-issue anti-snake bite serum, she did not get seriously sick.

Despite snake bite, guests from Saigon and rainy weather, I left NhaTrang on Friday following Christmas for a long anticipated ten day vacation. Vacationing is always fun and after five months of confining myself between hospital and town only four kilometers away, I was more than ready for it. But you must understand a few of the facts of travel in Vietnam before you can truly appreciate what an undertaking a short vacation is.

Fact 1. The security of road travel for an American, outside of a military convoy, is highly questionable in all areas; absolutely out of the question in most. That leaves air travel only.

Fact 2. All flights are subject to weather (it's currently rainy season in the northern half of South Vietnam, remember), ground fire from VietCong, the usual (and some unusual) repairs, sudden changes of the airline schedule by some V.I.P., civilian or military. So, schedules, if you can call them that, are so loose that flight delays are usually counted by days rather than minutes or hours.

Fact 3. Airport accommodations for the suddenly stranded are primitive. Worse still are the hotel accommodations in most cities which boost the economy via cyclo-drivers and prostitutes.

This was my outlook for vacation travel. But I soon realized that I had overlooked the most important fact of all.

Fact 4. There are more than 140,000 American military men in Vietnam, thousands more in civilian service of one kind or another. There are probably less than 1500 American women in Vietnam of whom I am one. Despite being surrounded by lovely Vietnamese women, almost without exception those American men are homesick for "round-eyed" women. To make a long story short, I had a lovely vacation with almost no difficulty in travel!

I spent six days vacationing in Hue, the northernmost city in South Vietnam. For centuries Hue was the home of the emperors of a united Vietnam and is still considered the Imperial City of the country. The only remaining examples of her former splendor, however, are slightly faded, Chinese-style temples and the beautiful and elaborate tombs of past monarchs which stand outside the city. Unfortunately, especially during rainy season, travel to most of these tombs is considered unsafe. So I had to be content with only brief views of some of the more minor tombs.

Hue is also considered the national center of Buddhism, which explains the frequent Buddhist protests centering there. The city also has several excellent institutions of higher learning which boast such illustrious alumni as Ho chi Minh and Nguyen Cao Ky. Vietnamese everywhere, whether or not they have visited Hue, extol the beauties of the city to a foreigner and it is common knowledge that the Perfume River and the girls of Hue are the most beautiful in the nation.

Vietnam Christian Service has seven people working in Hue on loan to World Relief Commission. Their project is an experimental/demonstration farm. Presently they are also developing a lay leadership training school. The main emphasis on the farm is garden produce, swine, and chickens. It made me feel very much at home to be looking over pigs and chickens again and to watch the grinding and mixing of livestock feed.

In a recent litter of pigs, they averaged ten pigs per sow and they now have fifty-two baby pigs which would do credit to any midwestern swine farm, I think. They do have their problems, however. The boar has shipping fever and the chickens have fowl-pox and there is no vaccine available for either just now.

It rained continuously the six days I spent in Hue and it was as cold as November in Ohio. So my sightseeing opportunities were limited. Instead, I shivered around the house most of the time bundled up in warm clothes I borrowed from the boys on the project. I wrote letters, read, puttered in the kitchen and struggled to grade a set of essay test papers in Vietnamese. That last futile activity I gave up after about five days! Evenings were spent at home playing pinochle or just visiting and several times we baked a pizza or popped corn, just like home.

After six days of this lovely relaxation I finally tore myself away and headed for Saigon. I was escorted by one of the boys from the Hue project who had to go to Saigon on business. Such a trip we had!

First we had to drive the fourteen kilometers out to the military airport at PhuBai because we decided to try to get a cargo plane. The road between Hue and PhuBai is not quite as secure as your front yard and there had been an early morning ambush along part of it. Apparently the driver of a U.S. military truck, which traveled that road shortly before we did, was as scared as I was, because he was driving too fast and hit a Vietnamese truck. It tied up traffic, including us, for more than an hour during which time we had to be well guarded by rifle-toting American MPs (military police).

In the process, of course, we missed our plane but finally caught an ARVN (Army of the Republic of Vietnam) air force cargo plane. After two hours of sitting on the runway at PhuBai, we went up to 19,000 feet to try to get out of the clouds and beyond ground fire range, then we went straight down into Danang, only forty-five minutes from PhuBai. It wasn't too comfortable with a stopped-up head in a non-pressurized cabin, but I survived.

After a few repairs to the plane, we left for Saigon having taken aboard one piano and about twenty Vietnamese passengers. This was a fascinating two hours filled with conversation with my Vietnamese neighbors over the roar of the C-47's engines which certainly didn't enhance my shoddy language skills. We also passed out airsick pills. Most of the time we were too late, and cargo planes don't have little plastic airsick bags! We collected extra clothes and towels to wrap around two tiny babies traveling with us, clad only in thin cotton shirts. They had begun to turn blue at such high altitudes. I was glad to touch down in Saigon at long last.

It's been over a year since I was last in Saigon. Prices are higher, the streets more crowded and noisy, but otherwise it is the same. It was good to see old friends, meet some of the new folks who have come and get some shopping done. But, as always, I was glad to leave again.

The trip home was a real experience. I was "co-pilot" in a single engine craft. I "helped navigate" by the map and listened in on the radio headphones. The view of the jungle and mountain terrain from the clear plastic bubble-shaped cockpit were breathtaking!

And so, after ten days of rest, I am back to work again. The new TB hospital has about eighteen patients in it already. A lower patient census in the hospital now in bad weather gives us a little time to clean and organize for the busy summer months ahead; to scare a few cockroaches and mice out of the cupboard corners; and to restock the shelves. The biggest medical event of this season will be the arrival of the first child of the Dr. Harold and Esther Kraybill. We are awaiting this any day now.

Thanks to so many of you for Christmas greetings and again I ask you to be patient in waiting for answers to your letters. The answer will come (I hope before next Christmas) but I can't guarantee when.

Sometimes the frustrations of language, culture, lack of appreciation, theft of supplies, inter-staff conflict, and just plain fatigue make it hard to remember why I'm here. But today as I watched U.S. fighter planes bombing a hillside south of NhaTrang, I thought of God's grief for each son and daughter, and I remembered!

9

In Frustrations

Newsweek
September 5, 1966

Chances of the Game

With unwonted candor, U.S. officials in Saigon disclosed last week that 160 South Vietnamese civilians and friendly troops were killed and 256 wounded—all unintentionally—by allied air strikes and artillery since July 1. Declared Gen. William C. Westmoreland, commander of U.S. forces in Vietnam: "We are sensitive to these incidents and want no more of them. If one does occur—mistake or accident—we intend to search it carefully for any lesson that will help us improve procedures and our controls."

The next mistake came less than 48 hours later during a pitched battle 55 miles north of Saigon between units of the U.S. First Infantry Division and a Viet Cong battalion. Two U.S. jets, aiming at smoke grenades marking Communist positions, missed their mark and instead dropped their canisters of napalm on the GI's—killing, according to the Associated Press, more than a score of them and wounding many more..

Grim Reports: Barely 50 yards away from where the canisters burst stood a CBS television team. Its leader, Canadian-born newsman Morley Safer, later radioed this grim report: "We hit the dirt. I put my head up and the jungle in front of us was on fire and running out of it were dozens of men, their clothes ablaze, some of them screaming, some rolling in the mud. In a moment, it was over. We reached them just as the medics were cutting away bits of skin and blackened uniforms. One boy of 19 kept asking, 'Why are they doing it? Tell them to stop.' Another trooper, his face a mass of blisters, his hair burned away, said softly through blackened lips: 'Goddam it, don't they know we're down here?' They brought the first sergeant in—it was a sight that was at once unbearable, yet held an awful fascination. His breath was a short rasp. The medic was attempting the 'kiss of life' through a rubber tube and then he died without a sound as we watched with helpless rage."

No less saddened than Safer was the First Infantry Division's commander, tough little Gen. William E. DePuy. He nevertheless took the tragedy with a veteran's resignation: "We are not angry at the Air Force. This was an error of only about 50 meters and [with planes going] at 200 knots, it can happen. It's the chances of the game."

January 19, 1967
NhaTrang

Dear Folks,

Could you to do a favor for me? Several weeks ago I told you that a friend had sent me $50 donated by the last BVS unit to be used in projects beneficial to the Vietnamese people. I've only managed to spend $7.50 of it so far. But one of the projects I've wanted to spend some of the money on is to buy a watch and a pair of bandage scissors.

I'd like to donate these to the three girls from the orphanage nearby who are studying the fundamentals of nursing in our training course. They will then be able to assist us in the medical care of the other orphans by treating minor cuts and bruises themselves. They have already studied bandaging but do not have scissors. They will soon be studying how to check pulses but do not have a watch.

I have looked all over NhaTrang and through the PX catalogue for a pocket watch but such is not available. Could you buy a relatively inexpensive pocket watch with a sweep hand, and send it to me? I will have it engraved with the name of the orphanage so that they know that it is not to belong to any one of them alone.

I asked a chaplain friend of mine if I could use his APO number for you to send it and he agreed willingly. So willingly did he agree, in fact, that he suggested that I have you pack it in some clothes or other things that I might need from home.

He will get me the scissors so all you would need to send is the watch, well packed in underwear and warm nightwear. He will be expecting a package with your return address on it so do not put my name anywhere on the outside of the package. That could get him in trouble. My conscience cannot rationalize such deception for just any little thing I want, but he has wanted to help me get the watch and this arrangement is as much his idea as mine.

You said that this month the special project in women's work at the church is Vietnam relief. If you haven't yet decided on a specific type of project I have a suggestion. If I have sent any pictures of hospital patients, you will see that some of them are wearing white pajama suits which are provided to them by the hospital. Many wear their own clothes but occasionally they need to be washed. At the present time we have enough pj tops to last about five more years but we are almost entirely out of bottoms. They are supposed to stay at the hospital and they are stamped with the hospital name. Even so they have a habit of walking off.

I am having some made for the immediate emergency out of print material that we got in the Vietnam relief packets. We will use some of the white for uniforms for our nurses and for surgical linens.

In the refugee camps where other VNCS units are working, the packets are usually left intact and given out to the Vietnamese women themselves. We also used these packets as our Christmas gifts to the hospital patients, adding candy, fruit, some writing materials, soap, and toothpaste. So the relief packets which we have received are very useful.

However, the pajama bottoms which I can make from the packets I have opened will only cover the present emergency. If the women's work could make some, you could send them to us through the church offices. Remember, however, that Vietnamese are not as big as Americans by a long shot. So I think that a boy's size fourteen to sixteen would be the best size since what we need are adult-sized pants. Smaller sizes would also be useful, although they are not needed as badly right now.

The Protestant clinic in Pleiku will be opening its inpatient division within a year. Therefore, if we don't need the pajama pants when they arrive perhaps Pleiku will. An inexpensive cotton material would be best; seersucker or crinkle crepe if it is available because it doesn't show wrinkles as badly. Colors such as blue or green or even mild prints would be acceptable and I don't think they would walk home quite as fast as white ones. Black is out because that would be just like they wear at home and there would be no way at all to keep them from being taken.

I had a lovely morning. I spent two hours playing a real live two-manual electric organ with pedal board and chimes. It is very much like the organ at church at home but I know even less about this one. It's a long story how I happened to be playing it.

The organ is in the American military chapel in Nha-Trang. They used to have a full time organist, one of the missionary wives, I understand. For some reason she had to give up the responsibility. The chapel is a large building but not especially well attended. The chaplain could not find anyone to replace her. He finally came to us almost in desperation. He hated to see such an organ go unused while the congregational singing suffered badly without it.

All this happened while I was on vacation. One of the nurses and one of the doctors who play a little agreed that we would provide music every Sunday until the chaplain could find someone permanently. The nurse played on Christmas Eve and the doctor played the past two Sundays. So now it is my turn.

I spent two glorious hours practicing this morning but it took all that time just to limber up my fingers and figure out the stops for the two manuals. I never did get around to trying the foot pedals. At any rate, it didn't sound as bad as I expected. I enjoyed it so much that I'd almost like to do it every Sunday. However, I work one Sunday a month.

More importantly, my conscience pricks me for attending military worship services as often as I do now. Every Sunday would be unbearable for my pacifist morals. The only English language services available on Sunday mornings are military services and there are times when I have to go to a religious service I can understand and feel a part of.

Distinctions between us and the military here in the field are not what people back home would consider ideal but it is almost impossible for us to disassociate with the military completely and still function. However, our first responsibility is to the Vietnamese in our work and personal contacts. So I'm left with many questions in my mind about playing the organ in the military chapel regularly, even though I enjoy it so much.

January 27, 1967
NhaTrang

Dear Folks,

Yesterday at siesta time, the dogs were making such an uproar at the back door of the doctor's house that I decided to get up and see what was wrong. There, on the steps, was a coiled snake, hissing and spitting at the barking dogs. Thank goodness for a front door! I ran out of it to the hospital as fast as I could and shouted for help. Anh Tin came and killed it with a broom. This country's wonders never cease!

Hospital census is down because of Tet, Vietnamese New Year, on February 9. We only have about twenty or twenty-five patients right now. The weather has been very warm the past three days. Maybe rainy season is behind us.

Newsweek
February 13, 1967

License Vs. Liberty

"At the present crucial juncture, we should have a free and decent press." When South Vietnamese Premier Nguyen Cao Ky unburdened himself of this unexceptionable statement in an after-dinner speech recently, his audience—which was composed of Saigon's leading editors and publishers—could scarcely believe its ears. . . .

Saigon never has had a free press, and commentary on the government or people in it has always been chancy. Government

censors have felt free to kill offending paragraphs or even entire
stories with only the vaguest of explanations. Just last month, a
three-column blank appeared on the front page of the English-
language Saigon Daily News. The censored material had been a
picture of Premier Ky stretched face down in the dirt the instant after
a mortar shell had misfired a few feet away from him. Another
English-language paper, the Vietnam Guardian, was once obliged
to run the daily column written by its managing editor, Ton That
Thien, with only its title, and Thien's by-line. The rest of the piece
consisted of white space. . . .

February 2, 1967
NhaTrang

Dear Family,
       What a special treat it is to get a letter partly written by my
dear, too-busy father. Pater, dear, your inquiries about the war
progress in this country remind me that my letters have been
sadly lacking in such information lately.
       Your available news coverage, inadequate as it is some-
times, is vastly better than ours. Several times a week we try to
buy a *Stars and Stripes,* the armed forces daily newspaper.
But the news it contains is slightly more biased than that
which you get in newspapers, and radio and TV there at
home. It is, however, fairly complete coverage of news both
here and around the world.
       Once a week we buy a *Time* and/or *Newsweek* but they
are often up to a month old. We can occasionally get news
broadcasts on armed forces radio, Radio Vietnam and, even
more occasionally, on Radio Manila or from Australia. Saigon
daily English language newspapers are biased and obviously
censored. It is a little beyond my present vocabulary to read a
Vietnamese paper even if it were regularly available.
       So, obviously, your knowledge of what is happening
here is much more complete than mine. I have read and
heard about the "clearing out" operations that have been
going on down in the delta, Operation Iron Triangle and
Cedar Falls, but I know little about what is actually going on. If I
believed everything I read and heard on armed forces news
media, I would not know why the war hadn't been won a long
time ago. The reporting of these current missions is similarly

one-sided. The best, most believable story I have been able to piece together so far is this:

Going into the rainy season which has now just passed, the VC were "hurting" a little more than previously in areas of supplies, food, medicines, and morale due to lack of any decisive victories. Desertions had been rising during November and December so, to increase morale, some U.S. military experts expected the VC to make an all-out, concentrated effort, regardless of cost in men or supplies.

The logical place for this push would be one of three places: 1) down from the demilitarized zone toward Hue and Danang because it would be the easiest area to move supplies and men into; also the VC would have the support of a greater percent of the population there; 2) across the center of the country at about the area of TuyHoa or north of there from the Cambodian border to the sea because the width of the country is narrow there: it would be the easiest place in which to cut the country in half which would be a tremendous psychological blow to the South Vietnamese; 3) a sweep into the delta region south of Saigon because it is the rice basket of the country: from there they could replenish their own supply. Also, a foothold south of Saigon, the capitol city, would be a terrible blow to the stability of the government there.

Christmas and New Year's saw slightly increased action in all three of these places. But, as of now, no open "broad daylight" VC push has been initiated. Everyone seems to agree that the VC are hurting but they've been fighting against great odds for a long time and they've no more reason to give up now than many times before.

I have been most interested in reading about your activities with various U.S. groups working for peace in this country. My conviction of the necessity for peace here as soon as possible is unchanged. But the longer I stay and the more of the situation here that I see, the more confused I get as to how or if this will ever be possible.

I'm not so sure that I could now speak with quite as much assurance about withdrawal of troops immediately and unconditional negotiations as I once could have. Everyone agrees that the war is a very bad thing for Vietnam. But the mutilation of home and family and the confiscation of property that some of my friends have experienced under Communism is not good either. Of course, murdering and confiscation in the name of protection also is not right. But is it really exhibiting a social conscience to just let such continue? Really I haven't been indoctrinated by the military: I'm just asking some questions that were much easier to answer at a distance.

Ideally, the people should decide for themselves by election what type of government they wanted, then abide by the majority opinion. However, politically, this country is still in infancy and, if this last election was any indication, a fair and just election is not easily come by.

So what's to be done? At this point, for me, all I can do is to pray, work and keep faith in the ultimate outcome of good in God's world. Although I do not know what the general opinion of the American public is at this time about the war, when I left the States it was not one hundred percent supportive of LBJ's conduct of it. I have faith that the soft-hearted American public will grow sick and tired of the fruitless slaughter here and begin to clamor loudly for the end of it.

Then, by negotiations or because of political improvements here, the American interest will begin to move out, leaving the entire country open to slow, patient, and relentless Communist influence. I wonder what will become of my good Catholic and Protestant Christian friends for whose religious views there will be no room under Communism. But, perhaps, if the pressure is taken off of him, Ho Chi Minh will develop a socialistic Yugoslavian-Russian communism and not a fanatical Chinese type. Perhaps there would be room for religious beliefs under such a tolerant form of Communism.

So continue to pray and work for peace in whatever ways you think right. Daily, I know more clearly that peace is God's intention; war is only an invention of humans which blocks the will of God.

These comments on military and political matters had better be kept for the eyes of the family only. Conceivably, I could get into a lot of trouble if they got very wide circulation.

So much for the political and military news. We made some news of our own this week. Saturday afternoon, after about eighteen hours of exhausting labor, the doctor's wife was delivered of an eight-pound baby boy by Caesarian section at the military hospital in NhaTrang.

She had wanted very much to deliver the baby here but, after a very good first stage of labor, it became obvious that the baby was too big and lying too transversely for her to move it down and deliver it normally. She continued to labor fruitlessly for another twelve hours. Finally both doctors here decided she'd better go in to the military hospital and be x-rayed.

While studying the films, the military doctors offered to admit her and do the C-section if necessary. Their offer was generously accepted. Both baby and mother are doing fine now and came home from the hospital today.

It will be a little different to have a wee one around this household after having it to ourselves for so long and doing as we pleased! I think that the Vietnamese are as pleased and proud of the baby as we are. They are fascinated by his blue eyes and blond hair and by the fact that already as a newborn he is as big as a three- or four-month-old Vietnamese baby. So now we are nine instead of eight.

For some reason I am a little homesick tonight. I didn't remember until I typed the date on this letter that tomorrow is Sis's birthday and I keep remembering all the times we used to get together to celebrate. One month from yesterday I will be half-finished with my term. The past year doesn't seem long but the coming one does!

February 9, 1967
DaLat

Dear Folks,

You wouldn't believe where this is being written. We're at DaLat attending a conference for all VNCS workers in the country. We're in the midst of giving our unit skit. It's supposed to be a typical unit meeting and what a circus! Doc has been writing on it for nights and we've been rehearsing it for several days. It's kind of hard to think of two things at once but I'm supposed to be writing letters.

February 13
NhaTrang

Back home again. The skit and the conference are in the past. The conference was exactly the shot-in-the-arm that I needed just now to fortify me for the days ahead. It was so good to see everybody and visit with so many people I hadn't seen for a long time. All the VNCS workers but three were there, a total of seventy. DaLat is very beautiful and, as always, it was rejuvenating to get away from the responsibilities of work for awhile. I'd say the conference was a roaring success even though I could only stay three of the six days.

Yesterday, the president of the hospital board and I spent most of the day coffin shopping, conducting a funeral, and burying a man from Cam Ranh/Ba Ngoi who died here at the hospital on Friday. He was Catholic, but the Catholics of the area were "too busy" to do anything to help his wife. They did give us a thousand piasters to buy a coffin.

We bought it and wrapped the body for burial. The president of the hospital board knew which palms to grease among the local officials in order to be able to buy a lot in the local Protestant cemetery. The Bible School students helped us dig a grave, carry the body to the cemetery, and conducted a fine Christian funeral. They then buried the man and helped me care for the wife until she was able to travel home again.

Some months ago a BVS unit sent me $50 (about five thousand piasters) to be used for unbudgeted expenses in helping Vietnamese people. I used some of it yesterday. I gave five hundred piasters to the Bible School students who, out of the kindness of their hearts, helped give a Christian burial to a stranger. Tomorrow I shall use some more to buy a bus ticket for an old man who has some sight back since eye surgery but no money to go home. And so it goes!

February 22, 1967
NhaTrang

My Dear Sisters,

You've all been sinfully neglected, haven't you? And I don't even know if this will be readable, but at least I tried!

This whole past month is just a haze in my memory. I can't remember time ever passing so quickly before. A month ago we spent an anxious weekend with the doctor and his wife as we took turns sitting with her through a difficult labor. Finally a C-section performed at the military hospital in NhaTrang produced an eight-pound boy. The next week was full of trips back and forth to the hospital in town to visit and help care for her. It didn't help at all that all three of our vehicles were out of commission.

This week all of the unit, except the doctor and his wife, went to DaLat for the Vietnam Christian Service holiday retreat held over Lunar New Year. Lunar New Year, or Tet, is really the big holiday of the year in Asia and I hated to miss celebrating it here at home. However, the conference was great.

DaLat is one of the most beautiful places in Vietnam with mountains, pine trees, and cold nights. The conference was six days of business, relaxation, and fellowship with all of our personnel around the country. I stayed for only three days because we couldn't leave the hospital unstaffed. So we had to take turns going to conference and staying at home to mind the "store." I really enjoyed those brief three days though.

Most of the time here at home and at work I get so caught up in, or I should say overwhelmed by, the problems and practical aspects of the job that the fine sounding theoretical considerations that brought me to this job are driven far from my mind and practice. Talking to other workers beset and frustrated by similar problems bolstered my sagging self and helped me to rediscover some of the ideals I had lost. I even retained some of those lofty ideals after I came back home—for about two days!

It took me a week after conference to get organized again in the hospital. The clinic was closed for ten days over Tet. Those first few days of normal schedule after the ten-day holiday were sheer chaos. It is now a week past that terrible week and I still do not really want to associate with people on my off-duty hours!

Thanks for the Valentine. I needed that!

February 26, 1967
NhaTrang

Dear Folks,

Our long anticipated short-term eye specialist arrived last Saturday and immediately went to work. That means three to four cases of surgery six mornings a week and a jam-packed eye clinic every afternoon in addition to our regular clinic five mornings of the week and our usual inpatient load. To make matters more confusing, two of our three inter-preters have recently left us. One of our nurses is still on vaca-tion; another had to leave for a special conference in Saigon leaving only two western nurses here. And last weekend we had our two doctors, the eye specialist, and two visiting doc-tors all trotting around the hospital writing orders and asking questions. Things are a little better now with only four doc-tors, and the vacationing nurse is back among us.

March 9, 1967
NhaTrang

Dear Folks,

It's been a long time, hasn't it? As always I plead "busy-ness." The usual work load continues as well as a large hospi-tal census and all the extra eye work being done by the visiting surgeon.

Maintaining this kind of a schedule resulted in my catch-ing two diseases: a minor bronchitis and laryngitis which I'm still coughing out, and a major depression (the worst since I've come), which I'm still trying to shake off. I guess it resulted from a combination of approaching birthday, overwork, fatigue, "anniversary reaction," hot tempers among the unit, and this developing chest cold. But I got close enough to the end of my rope that I had to tie a knot in it and go looking for someone to help me back up.

Never in my life have I felt such a complete, sickening loneliness and isolation. I felt almost physically sick. So I went to the office of a military chaplain friend of mine and had myself a good therapeutic cry on his shoulder. He just heard me out; all about fatigue, overwork, inability to talk with any of the unit group about problems, conflicts with my housemate, frustrations of being forced by environment to give poor nursing care, inability to work through the language barrier, my guilt feelings at my inability to live up to the noble theories which brought me here, my feelings of difference and inferiority to my coworkers, my sudden acute loneliness and, finally, the seeming impossibility of surviving another year of this, let alone working effectively.

His suggestions were only two: a complete physical exam soon and, after a period of rest, considering whether to terminate my service early. I'll have the physical exam next week but I have not yet entirely put out of my mind the possible necessity of terminating early.

I extended my term for one reason only: I thought I could do better work the second year than the first. So far it's been as bad if not worse. In view of my reasons for being here, I feel like a complete failure. But, on the other hand, what's there to come home to? Can culture shock last this long?

I'm really excited to be so close to the work the eye surgeon is doing. Surgery is not my thing but I have helped a little and it is fascinating. Patient rounds yesterday illustrated some of the marvelous progress being made. Doc removed the dressing from an eye which had been blind for many years before the surgery. Doc held up several fingers and, to test the level of returned sight, asked the patient how many fingers he saw. In almost reverent voice, the patient replied, "The doctor has a beard!"

My English classes are going well and I simply love teaching them. I'm more relaxed and get more sense of reward teaching than I ever have in nursing. So, you see, not everything is black but I had to be honest or I couldn't write at all. If I didn't write, you'd know something was wrong and not know what it was.

I'll not be writing a newsletter for awhile because the only interesting subject I could write about non-hypocritically just now would be the "frustrations of volunteer service abroad." Say, that's not a bad topic. Maybe I will. But I'd better wait until I can view the frustration from a better perspective, like sitting on top of my sense of humor, not buried under it as I am now!

March 16, 1967
NhaTrang

Dear Folks,

Praise the Lord! I survived both the cold and the depression and I am almost back to normal again. I told the unit members here that a little earnest prayer, a quarter grain of Phenobarbital and ten hours of sleep can work wonders. I'm still trying to keep up on the sleep and the prayer!

I think I'm almost straightened out enough to try writing another edition of the newsletter. I hope it will follow soon. I got birthday cards from several unexpected people. I'm sure that helped brighten my mood.

Work continues as before, a leg-wearing and patience-stretching endurance exercise. Clinic is like a three-ring circus most of the time, trying to run separate medical and eye clinics in one room the size of our kitchen at home.

Marcy leaves for her out-of-country vacation next week. That takes our most experienced clinic screening nurse out and I don't know what we'll do then. I'd rather like to work in clinic a little but so far she hasn't mentioned a word about it. She acts as though I were entirely incapable of even trying to do "her job" so I won't open myself to the possibility of her ridicule by asking.

Right now, more than ever before, I'm needed in the hospital. With eye surgery every day we have a very strict post-surgical routine to carry out for cataract patients. We also have so many outpatients waiting around for surgery that once every day or so I have to go around just asking people who they are and trying to match them to a record some place. With three doctors making rounds, writing orders and doing procedures at various times, the whole thing is more of an exercise in memorization than for nursing ability.

It's really very exciting and interesting. Two days ago the visiting eye surgeon did a corneal transplant and he will repair a detached retina as soon as we get a diathermy machine. Probably nowhere else in this country outside of Saigon are such things being done.

There is humor as well as excitement involved in the eye surgery. The corneas which the eye surgeon transplanted belonged to our laundry lady here at the hospital. She was a middle-aged woman who died rather suddenly and unexpectedly the beginning of the week. She and her family are Christians, members of the local Protestant Church. When the eye doctor explained to them, through an interpreter, about the possibility of using her corneas for transplant so that another person could see better, her husband agreed to the procedure.

The corneas were "harvested" and transplanted to two Vietnamese patients. Even though the donor was Vietnamese, since it was the American doctor who was doing the surgery, the word that got around among our hospitalized patients and their families was that now those patients receiving the corneas would have one brown eye and one blue eye and they would be able to read English! I hope the recipients weren't too disappointed when they found this rumor wasn't true.

For the past week or so I've been having trouble getting anything done in free time except reading. I've rediscovered the joys of this fine art and I spend nearly every evening immersed in a book, knowing that I should be writing letters or hospital reports or planning hospital improvements. Instead I spend the time in *The Screwtape Letters, The Bridges of Toko-Ri, Here I Stand, How to Become a Bishop Without Being Religious, The Group,* and *O Ye Jigs and Juleps.* Just now I'm forcing myself to put down *Company of the Committed* which I find truly fascinating.

Last Sunday, for a change, Lance Woodruff, another VNCSer who is visiting here from Saigon, went with me to Catholic mass down the beach at a fishing village from which we get many patients. We walked about three kilometers down paths and byways I didn't know existed to get there. The service was interesting but completely unintelligible to me. I could understand part of the Vietnamese, part of the Latin, and part of the ritual but not very much of any one of the three. We did, however, see several old friends and patients there at the church.

Summer is almost upon us again. The temperature is rising daily and the sea is beginning to feel good at long last

after the long chilly rainy season. This is the nicest time of the
year, I think. It's warm but not yet parched. In another month
or two the grass will begin to get brown and the sun really
begins to scorch about five or six hours of the day.

March 24, 1967
NhaTrang

Dear Friends,
    Having just survived a depression of major import even
for me, I feel called upon, and eminently qualified, to
enlighten you with some of the truths it has revealed to me.
The subject of these truths is one which has long occupied
much of my time and attention. But it is only now, refortified
with my normal sense of humor, that I dare to set these considerations before you, my friends, who trust so naively in the
"good work" I am doing. And so, the subject of this epistle is
"The frustrations of foreign service," or "What the recruitment propaganda never tells you!" I don't want to disillusion
anyone aspiring to the diplomatic corps but the skeletons in
my closet deserve an airing.
    Life here, in general, consists of work and leisure time.
Frustration can be considered accordingly. Take work, for
example. "How are you?" and "May I help you?" are handy
stock phrases for a nurse in ascertaining a patient's condition. As far as I know, there is no adequate Vietnamese
equivalent for either phrase.
    Every word said to or heard from a patient or family
member, whether it is reassurance or reprimand, taking a
case history or taking a temperature, must be done in Vietnamese or through an interpreter. An interpreter must be
hunted down, brought up front from the busy clinic, talked to,
listened to, the problem settled as quickly as possible and the
interpreter returned to clinic.
    If the communication is made in Vietnamese, it must be
made only in my very limited vocabulary or else translated
from my poor Vietnamese into good Vietnamese by one of
my nurses. Then, what the patient says must be translated
back into my poor vocabulary before anything can begin to

be done. A person could die before this procedure gets completed!

Language is the biggest problem but there are others. The word "shortage" covers several of them. For fifty inpatients, fifty TB patients, an outpatient clinic of 150 daily and, at present, forty eye surgery patients, we have a staff of three MDs (one an eye surgeon here for two months), four Western nurses, two interpreters, one trained Vietnamese nurse, seven other in-service trained Vietnamese workers, two cleaning workers, and one laundry lady.

Five of the seven in-service trained workers are fifteen to seventeen years old and have little more sense of responsibility than an American of the same age. By that I mean it's difficult for them to remember even routine jobs without being reminded; impossible for them to undertake jobs on their own initiative. I feel we've made real progress, however, because now they usually remember the bath and treatment schedule. Lately they've been remembering, for two whole days at a time, some point upon which I have practiced my increasingly fluent "angry Vietnamese vocabulary" on them. It makes them lose face but it certainly saves me an ulcer.

We have other shortages, too, such as beds and linens. At present there are five patients on the floor on the front porch and three on cots in the hall. Two months ago we had enough grass mats and linens for fifty patients. Now, some patients are on blankets on the bare floor because perhaps ten percent of the earlier patients helped themselves to the mats or a piece of linen upon which was stamped the name of the hospital in large black letters.

You can't really blame them. They think like the little boy whom we called back last week as he went swinging down the hospital lane on his way home. He had his discharge medicines in one hand and *Chan-Y-Vien Tin-Lanh* stamped boldly across the seat of the pants he was wearing. "But," his father protested as we firmly removed the pants, "he has only one pair of pants and they're so dirty." I was about to take pity on him when I remembered the week before.

In similar pity, I gave a little gown to a mother for her freshly bathed baby to replace the dirty rags we had removed from him. Within three hours, five other women in the hospital produced babies in dirty clothes begging and pleading for a gown. Several of the babies I had seen previously in clothes better than I had to offer. But anything will sell on the black market.

I had to explain, as I always do, that we are not a relief and material aid center and we do not have enough supplies for our own patients, let alone to give away. "But I am only one and the doctor is so rich," they invariably say. If it is the first or second time of the day, I patiently repeat the explanation. If it is the third to the tenth time, I repeat it. Beyond the tenth time, I simply shake my head, say "no," and walk away feeling like a cruel but trapped beast!

There are also frustrations of overabundance. Take dirt and insects, for example. Seldom does any wound or laceration heal without infection. Surgical infections, however, are inexplicably rare considering our pressure cooker autoclave and our special operating room fly swatter.

Currently we have a serious burn case: a fifteen-year-old girl whose blouse caught fire when she was cooking. She rolled in the dirt to put out the fire and probably saved her life. But she was left with third degree burns across her entire front chest and upper arms which were caked with dirt when we first saw her. Despite all the cleaning measures we could institute, she developed an infection. Now we're trying to keep her under continuous saline compresses which seem to clean and debride it little by little, but flies and ants are a constant nuisance around her bed. I think we're winning that battle with a mosquito net, insect spray, and water cans under the legs of the bed. I don't know what will become of her, however, for we have not yet located a workable dermatome, a special knife needed for skin grafting.

Also in the realm of overabundance is the gift of soap which we received from an Army chaplain friend last week. When he offered us some surplus PX soap, we were most appreciative because so many of the skin problems we see daily are simply complications of common filth. Little did we realize, however, in what quantities the American army deals. Even their surplus is beyond comprehension.

The next day, up our little driveway, came three huge Army trucks, one with a mounted hydraulic lift and the other two loaded with metal containers as big as small storage rooms. Those metal containers held approximately 80,000 bars of soap, slightly damaged but usable. They now adorn our back yard!

Another frustrating overabundance is uninvited assistance in medical therapy from patients, family, friends, neighbors, and strangers. Let me hasten to explain. We ask every patient to have one person stay with patients to help with such things as cooking for and feeding them, giving fluids, bathing, notifying the nurses of pain, bleeding, or other changes in condition. They are our special duty nurses and we couldn't do without them.

What we could do without is their practice of Vietnamese folk medicine (sometimes called Chinese medicine) before or during the time they have brought the patient to us for our brand of medicine. Don't get me wrong. The practice of Vietnamese medicine is a fine art. But, folk medicine doesn't mix with our feeble attempts toward improving the health of our patients.

One of the most common and, fortunately, most innocuous practices is the sniffing of, or massaging the affected part with, oil of wintergreen or camphor. I am definitely in favor of this practice as it provides useful occupational therapy for family members who otherwise would be idle, worried, and helpless. It also markedly improves the odor of the patient's surroundings.

There are, however, other practices. For the relief of pain, for example, there are two common practices. A series of parallel knife cuts or the application of a heated suction apparatus over the affected part is supposed to draw out the pain. Besides the obvious disadvantages of additional pain and unattractive bruise marks for two or three weeks, these practices create additional problems for a patient with liver disease and poor blood clotting ability.

But, for me, the most heartbreaking practice of Vietnamese folk medicine is the not uncommon belief that a sick baby should not be fed. Milk, many of the more superstitious mothers feel, causes diarrhea even in a healthy baby. One with diarrhea or vomiting is often not given even water for days at a time. The original gastroenteritis is then complicated by dehydration and near starvation if the baby lives that long.

Last night a baby died who had apparently survived about a month without food and several days without water. It had been taken to the Province Hospital in NhaTrang but had been taken home without permission three days later because "it wasn't well yet." Finally, it came to us: a four year old whose forearms were about as big around as my middle finger and whose eyes were vacant and clouded over by a film because he was too weak to blink them.

He was beyond crying, beyond reacting to pain, beyond any response except occasionally grinding his poor, rotten teeth. Despite our poor efforts to save the child, it died. I found it un-Christianly difficult to hold my temper with the mother who seemed convinced that the baby died because we fed it milk!

This document has already reached a length I never dreamed of and I haven't begun my dissertation on free-time frustrations. To prevent all of you from succumbing to either eyestrain or boredom I'll leave that till the next chapter in this travelogue.

10

In Culture Shock

Newsweek
February 6, 1967

Leave The Driving To Us

There is no rail travel. The Viet Cong have long since seen to that. River traffic is as hazardous as it is unpredictable. Travel by motor car is only at the risk of one's life, and air travel is so expensive and so heavily booked that only the very rich or the very patient can afford it. But despite the size and scope of these roadblocks, people in war-torn South Vietnam still come and go from place to place. There is harassment aplenty, cabled NEWSWEEK correspondent Francois Sully, but salesmen continue to make their rounds, children in Saigon visit parents in the countryside, and the economic life of the nation somehow goes on. All of this is thanks to South Vietnam's 15,000-vehicle nationwide bus service and the nerveless drivers who man them on a transport network whose perils have not been matched anywhere since the days of the Burma Road. . . .

"This is a rough-and-tumble business," said driver Hai Van, in eloquent understatement. To many of the drivers, 80 miles an hour on a congested highway is a crawl, and every morning, along the well-traveled roads leading out of Saigon, the nearby paddies are dotted with overturned buses, their cargoes of livestock and people scattered across the landscape. . . .

April 5, 1967
Nha Trang

Dear Folks,

Again just a note to let you know that I'm alive. But this time that is not an idle jest! Since you don't operate on the principle that "no news is good news," I thought I'd better write the whole story to you before you hear it from some grapevine source well embellished.

I think I wrote you earlier about our new Honda 50 motorscooter. Shortly after we got it I took off for town on it to do some shopping and errand running. It's a real joy to drive and I was consciously being as careful as possible and keeping my speed down. I set fifteen mph as my upper limit.

I got along just fine until I was on my way home. I remember a military jeep behind me that was going too fast and tooting his horn at everybody to get out of his way. I remember seeing the bus that belongs to the Bible School coming toward me followed by the car of the president of the hospital board, Pastor Nam. I vaguely remember the jeep trying to pass between me and the Bible School bus and thinking to myself, "He's too close."

I don't remember anything else except crying and hearing Mrs. Nam talk to me. Finally I opened my eyes under a surgical face drape with Doc humming a popular song as he stitched up my face. I started crying again but Doc said, "Quit wiggling or you'll mess up my suture job." When I discovered that I could move all my arms and legs I wasn't so scared any more. Then I was told that the new Honda was still in perfect running order and I could relax completely and let them finish the job of patching me up. While they did, I tried to piece together what had happened.

What I have written above is all I can remember. Carl got most of the rest of the story from Pastor and Mrs. Nam; what a blessing that they were there!

None of us is sure whether or not the jeep actually hit me. I don't remember any impact at all but obviously something happened and the jeep just speeded up and kept going. A Korean jeep followed him, got his number and discovered that the driver is an officer at the military academy just down the beach from our hospital. It is possible that he did not hit me but that I turned so sharply to miss him that I lost my balance.

At any rate, the abrupt change of direction or an impact threw me forward and the left side of my face, about at eye level, hit the mirror on the left handlebar of the Honda, breaking it off the scooter. That was the only damage to the scooter and Carl was able to drive it home.

I must have completely knocked myself out at that time. The left lens of my glasses was broken out but there was no damage directly to the eye. I now have about ten stitches above the eye and three below to close the gash that was there but the eye itself seems OK.

The scooter apparently skidded and fell on its left side, and so did I. My left elbow, right knee, left shoulder and hip, and right hand appear to have taken the brunt of my fall. None of these areas required suturing but they are covered with painful and very dirty friction burns.

Pastor and Mrs. Nam stopped immediately when they saw that an accident had happened, not knowing who the victim was. Before they could get to me, two women had come out from their houses nearby and were trying to sit me up. This is rather unusual for most Vietnamese are not noted for their concern for strangers. However, these were two Buddhist ladies, Mrs. Nam said, who had been to the clinic here and knew who I was. Of course I remember none of this as I was knocked out like the loser in a championship fight.

The four of them managed to pick me up and put me in the back of the Bible School bus and bring me to the hospital. I guess I created quite a stir when I arrived! I wouldn't know about that but I do know that I was glad to hear Doc singing instead of a heavenly (or otherwise) choir. I was relieved to see that the anxious faces of my white-robed Vietnamese nurses were not backed by wings!

After the suturing, our visiting eye surgeon said he didn't think that I had lost a nickel's worth of beauty. I said it was probably because I hadn't had that much to start out with! When the last bandage was secured, I very slowly and hesitantly tried connecting my feet with the floor. They worked, except for the right knee and I walked over to the house under my own power, surrounded by curious patients and staff.

After a fairly restful night I got up this morning with pains in places I didn't know I had, brush burns in many odd places and a somewhat swollen and discolored left eye. I'm really a little disappointed that I don't have a full blown shiner to show off! I took the day off and rested most of the time but I think perhaps I can work part-time tomorrow.

A number of people stopped in today to visit and I can assure you that grateful prayers have been said on this side of the Pacific. Many more should be said on that side after you read this. But, all in all, stiff and sore, I'm as good as can be expected and better than I had feared. Console yourselves with that and the fact that apparently it was not my fault in any way. That makes the pain a little easier to bear.

Well, I guess that's enough of a bombshell for now. But remember, by the time you read this, the accident is long past and I'm halfway healed already. It's too late to worry about it. I promise to continue to be careful and to pray for undeserved protection for the times other people are not!

April 11, 1967
NhaTrang

Dear Folks,

I'm healing well, almost without scars except for a permanently cleft left eyebrow. I'm thankful that it's not the eye that was cut but I'm a little sad every time I look in the mirror or winkle up my forehead. Doc says if it doesn't improve in the next month or two he'll do a little plastic repair and pull the edges of the scar together so it will not be so noticeable.

It will take several weeks to get my glasses fixed and I must check about getting a chipped tooth capped. Otherwise, I'm almost as good as new.

I decided not to try to trace the jeep because we didn't have the full number and it would be a case of his word against mine. Then I'd have to admit that I was unconscious. Besides, in a traffic accident involving Americans and Vietnamese, usually the Americans end up paying. I could get homesick for the American legal system.

Last Sunday was a nice day. Dave, one of the IVSers, invited several of us to go out with him, visit his project, and have lunch with some friends of his, Buddhist nuns in a small convent near the village where he works. I took lots of pictures which will be coming to you. Look for several pictures of small women with shaved heads dressed in flowing saffron-yellow robes.

Their religious devotion is truly remarkable. They are strict vegetarians but the food they served us was delicious. They could not eat with us, however, because they only eat once a day, in the morning before the sun comes up.

We looked around the convent. They farm and raise most of their own fruits and vegetables. We visited their religious shrine and talked with them a little. With a Vietnamese vocabulary confined mostly to "Where does it hurt?" and "How long have you been sick?" it is a little difficult to carry on proper social conversation. But we tried, and we smiled and used sign language a lot! They indicated that some of their friends from the nearby village had received care at Chan-Y-Vien Tin-Lanh in the past. They were generous in their thanks to us for the good care they had received and they were most gracious hostesses for our visit.

On the way home we looked in on some of the other projects our IVS friend is involved in: a peanut oil factory, his mushroom farm, charcoal kiln, and others. It was the farthest north of town that I had ever driven since I arrived. Perfectly safe in the daytime, I guess.

Sunday evening we were invited by the hospital board to a feast in honor of the departure of our short-term eye surgeon. It was held in a restaurant in NhaTrang and was a delightful meal. We enjoyed visiting with such illustrious company.

Well, I'm meeting a friend for lunch in NhaTrang so I'd better get on my way. Today is the first time I've been brave enough to take a vehicle out alone since my mishap last week. I'm taking the car instead of the scooter!

April 20, 1967
NhaTrang

Dear Folks,

Enclosed you will find a slide picture of a Korean master sergeant. It's a long story but, before I start telling you the story and forget the errand, let me ask: will you have a print made of this picture and return it to me as quickly as possible? You may keep the slide at home.

Now the story about M/Sgt. Park. About three weeks ago, Ruth was driving our Land Rover which is vintage 1946 or so and looks like something out of an African safari movie. She was headed to town and, along a particularly narrow and heavily traveled stretch of road, somebody up ahead made an abrupt stop. This created a chain reaction among the following vehicles which were, as always, too closely bunched together.

Her car hit the Vietnamese Army truck ahead then settled back as his vehicle moved ahead a little. She was then smacked from behind by a Korean army truck which pushed her into the truck ahead again. Traveling slowly as they were, no one was hurt and the army trucks were not even scratched. The Land Rover, however, suffered moderate accordion injuries. As usual the driver of the Vietnamese truck didn't even stop to investigate the accident that he had, in part, created. The Koreans did.

Carl and I happened along a little later on our way to town and we stayed around for the fun; about three and a half hours of it! Naturally, the Koreans spoke neither English nor Vietnamese and we did not speak Korean. So they began to flag down passing Korean jeeps until we had what seemed like about a quarter of the Republic of Korea's army there milling around our vehicles.

Officers appeared from everywhere; interpreters materialized miraculously—English, Vietnamese, Chinese, French—everything except Korean! Photographers were here and there and, in the middle, stood our little nurse and the driver of the Korean vehicle. He maintained that he had stopped completely before she hit him so hard that she bounced herself forward. She did not agree.

M/Sgt. Park, who is pictured on the enclosed slide, was the chief interrogator of the accident. The Koreans were very kind, courteous, respectful, and helpful but firm in their demands to know which of the damages to our car had been caused by their truck and which by the Vietnamese truck. She could not say definitely, of course, so the investigation took a very long time.

I was going about here and there trying out my new camera when M/Sgt. Park asked me to take a picture of him. Of course I did and also complimented him on how handsome a picture it would make. His men quietly made the suggestion that I get a print made and give it to him. That's what I would like for you to do for me. Our "Asian-style" courtesy must have worked because the outcome of it all was that the Koreans agreed to fix the vehicle entirely and did not charge us anything. Our Paxman/mechanic said it wasn't fixed quite as well as he had hoped but it did run. Please send the picture back as soon as possible in case M/Sgt. Park is due to get shipped back to Korea soon.

I conclude that either letters are being lost in the mail again or you people are keeping so busy that you're not at home to receive them when they come. I have yet to receive from you any acknowledgement of a letter I sent nearly two weeks ago in which I recounted my unfortunate mishap with our Honda. It's ancient history now and the wounds have healed fairly satisfactorily. It still puts me in a foul mood to study my face in the mirror, however, and my knees look like I have leprosy since the scars remaining there will not suntan. I've not ridden the Honda since. In fact, I've not ridden on a scooter at all. I simply must work up the nerve, at least, to ride with someone else driving.

As I mentioned in a previous letter, I hardly can find time for work or letter writing these days, so fascinated am I by some of the reading I am doing. *Living Letters* and the *New English Translation of the New Testament* are as engaging as a contemporary novel. In the wee hours of this morning I finished reading *Out of the Jaws of the Lion* by Homer Dowdy who also wrote *Bamboo Cross,* the story of the early missionary efforts with the tribes people of Vietnam.

Out of the Jaws of the Lion is a fascinating book about the trials of missionaries to the Congo during the time of the Simba rebellion. I could see many parallels to the situation in

Vietnam. The conflict in Vietnam is on a higher intellectual and cultural plane but there is the same hungry quest for power and the same contemptuous attitude to moral, social, or personal considerations.

I do not personally know any Christians or missionaries who have suffered under the VietCong. No, I take that back. The first husband of the Western missionary lady who previously lived in the house where my housemate and I now reside was killed by the VC at a roadblock near Banmethuot.

But I am sure that many now serving in this country, both Western and Vietnamese Christians, would have such a faith as Dowdy describes in the Congo if and when they were called upon to exhibit it. A few years ago I would have scoffed at such a simple, blind, almost fatalistic faith as he describes in the missionaries who faced death for themselves and their loved ones. But the older I get the more I learn how important it is, especially in our age of unbelief, to believe in *something*. The strong people of every age have been those who have believed in something, be it Hitler, God, the theory of relativity, the pursuit of knowledge, Communism, women's sufferage or whatever. Their faith gave them substance, confidence, courage and a direction to go in seeking out tasks to do to further their faith.

Another book through which I am slowly working my way is Dag Hammerskjöld's *Markings*. It is not the sort that you sit down and read in one evening or two or in a week or a month for that matter. I find I must read it in pieces which sometimes takes weeks to digest.

The introduction to the book is as deep but more understandable than the book itself. It is written by W. H. Auden who is himself a poet and writer. His introduction is essential to the book and to an understanding of the man who wrote it.

There is one passage which intrigues me especially as I suppose I identify with it. He is attempting to describe Hammerskjöld's personality. I quote in part (with many omissions to make my point):

"To the outward eye Dag Hammerskjöld's career was, from beginning, one of uninterrupted success . . . Inwardly, however, in spite of all of these advantages—in part, perhaps, because of them—there is spiritual distress. The portrait of the up and coming young man that emerges from the earlier pages of *Markings* is of one of those 'unsymmetric' natures which can all too easily come to grief.

"[His was] an exceptionally aggressive superego . . . which demands that a Hammerskjöld shall do and be better than other people; on the other hand, (he had) an ego weakened by a 'thorn in the flesh' . . . Consequently a feeling of personal unworthiness. . . .

"Further, though endowed with many brilliant gifts, (Hammerskjöld was) not, I think, a genius, not, that is to say, a person with a single overwhelming talent and passion for some particular activity . . .which determines, usually early in life, exactly what his function on earth is to be. . . .

"To be gifted but not to know how best to make use of one's gifts, to be highly ambitious but at the same time to feel unworthy, is a dangerous combination which can often end in mental breakdown or suicide and . . . the thought of suicide was not strange to Hammerskjöld. . . .

"Long before he discovered a solution Hammerskjöld knew exactly what his problem was—if he was not to go under he must learn how to forget himself and find a calling in which he could forget himself—and knew that it was not in his own power to do this. The transition from despair over himself to faith in God seems to have been a slow process, interrupted by relapses. Two themes came to preoccupy his thoughts. First, the conviction that no man can do properly what he is called upon to do in this life unless he can forget his ego and act as an instrument of God. Second, that for him personally, the way to which he was called would lead to the Cross, i.e., to suffering, worldly humiliation and the physical sacrifice of his life." (pg. xiii to xvi, *Markings,* Dag Hammerskjöld. New York: Alfred A. Knopf, 1964.)

The contents of the book are mostly rather poetic and difficult to understand. This, however, is crystal clear and strikes me deeply.

Well, I must do some sewing this afternoon. The hospital is out of pillow cases again. The doctor's wife and I just made twenty-five about a month ago out of some of the print material that had been sent to us in those special Vietnam refugee bundles. But they were so pretty that they've disappeared already. I'll try once more and if they walk off again I guess I'll have to go back to plain old drab white ones!

April 23, 1967
NhaTrang

Dear Folks,

Just a note again to keep you in touch with the rotten streak of luck I've fallen into. I've been in bed continuously since Saturday afternoon with headache, sore throat, and soaring temperatures. This morning is the first time my temp has been normal in three days. It's been running 100 in the morning, 101 in the afternoon, and 102 at night. If I had tonsils I'd think I had tonsillitis. That's just what it feels like. It's a good sign that the temperature is coming down this morning so maybe I'll try to work a little this afternoon. As rotten as I felt this weekend it wasn't hard to stay in bed while others worked, but it made me feel darn guilty!

April 27, 1967
NhaTrang

Dear Folks,

Finally, after about three weeks, I can say I feel really good physically again! After two days of pain all over, four days of sore knees, a week and a half of pain around the eye, five days of a boil on my chin, three days of sore throat, one day of toothache, and several hours of belly cramps yesterday, today is lovely! I don't hurt any place and I feel great. This has been a string of bad luck that I hope is over now.

You deserve a little more information about the toothache. About one-third of my lower rear molar on the left side dropped out last week. It was probably broken off in the accident with the Honda. Tuesday of last week I went into NhaTrang and had it filled by a Vietnamese dentist, free, but without any anesthetic of any kind.

I keep forgetting to mention to you that about two months ago a book was published by a nurse who formerly worked here at Chan-Y-Vien Tin-Lanh. The book, titled *Lucky-Lucky* is by Marva Hasselblad and is about her experiences as the only nurse here at the clinic from 1962 to 1965. There are a few pictures in the book also and you might find it interesting. We have a copy here but I have not read it yet. I'm afraid that reading about the past glories of the place would depress me! If you could buy a copy and send it to me I would give it to Ba Ba, the cleaning lady pictured in the book.

With an expanded staff we've had to build a new house to accommodate us all. It's a few yards north of the doctor's house back from the beach a little further. I guess we'll be moving in as soon as the pump gets installed. It's a nice house but it doesn't have the view we have now.

The nursing school is a real possibility for this coming August. My first course will be microbiology. How I wish now for those two textbooks lying there at home on the shelf. But it's not worth the dollars or the effort to sent them. We're finding a few (precious few) available here but, thank goodness, it's not going to be a very advanced course.

May 6, 1967
NhaTrang

Dear Folks,

I guess I'm finally getting over all my illnesses but I'm still working on getting rid of a series of boils on my chin which have plagued me for about three weeks. Apparently I ground some dirt into my chin when I had the Honda accident. It is very resistant to antibiotics and warm soaks and has been rather painful until today. The doctor opened the boils a little last night and they are draining now.

I feel a little like Job and I have neither his patience nor his faith. I'm just sick and tired of being sick and tired! The weather is getting beastly hot just as I remember it was last year when I first arrived here in NhaTrang. It was one year ago today, to be exact.

We got moved into the new house yesterday. It's quite nice and rather more civilized than the little house where I lived before, except that it doesn't have water, screens, curtains, or much furniture yet. I'll try to include some pictures of it on my next roll of film and have it sent home to you.

Speaking of pictures, on the film I am presently finishing there is a picture of a two-pound premature infant in our makeshift box and light bulb incubator. The baby, the only child of its parents, died the next day. After several anxious days, we took the mother in to the Province Hospital in Nha-Trang for abdominal surgery. There they discovered that she had two large ovarian cysts which are probably malignant. The father very much wants a picture of that baby. So please, as quickly as you can after you get the film, have a print made and send it back.

Well, it's almost bedtime and although tomorrow is Sunday I must work as usual. That means getting up fairly early.

Newsweek
June 5, 1967

The Trouble In I Corps

Another truce—this one in honor of Buddha's birthday—came and went in Vietnam last week, and when full-scale military operations resumed, little, if anything, seemed to have changed. In Saigon, the U.S. command grimly announced that 337 Americans had been killed and 2,282 wounded the preceding week. These figures—a new high for the war—primarily reflected intense fighting between U.S. marines and North Vietnamese regulars in the southern half of the Demilitarized Zone separating the two Vietnams... And though the marines early last week withdrew on schedule from the DMZ after what was described as a highly successful sweep of enemy base camps, about 2,000 leathernecks soon found themselves forced to dash back in to quench a murderous shower of artillery and mortar fire from a hilltop somehow still occupied by Communist troops.

At stake in the bloody battles in the DMZ was not the zone itself but a much more valuable prize—the five northern provinces of South Vietnam, known as I Corps after the South Vietnamese Army unit nominally entrusted with their defense. In the costly contest for I Corps, the North Vietnamese Army has shown itself perfectly willing to sacrifice whole companies and even battalions if, in return, it can inflict severe losses on the marines. And with dismaying frequency, the Communists have succeeded in doing just that.

As a result of their mounting casualties (50 percent of the leathernecks committed to the battle near Khe Sanh a month ago were either killed or wounded), the marines have come in for blister-ing criticism from their colleagues in the other services. Thus, it was not altogether surprising when the Pentagon recently announced that Lt. Gen. Lewis W. Walt, the top Marine commander in Vietnam, was being transferred to a Washington desk job starting this week. Said one leathery Marine gunnery sergeant: "This is the most frus-trating war the Marine Corps ever fought. We are fighting for our very reputation." . . . .

June 20, 1967
BaoLoc, Lam Dong Province

Dear Friends,

Three months ago I promised to continue with the second chapter of "The Frustrations of Foreign Service," or "What the Recruitment Propaganda Never Tells You." This installment will be devoted to leisure time frustrations. You will recall I gave a rather thorough coverage to the frustration of work in the last edition. And, at the present time, I find myself in a situation which lends itself perfectly to the dissertation at hand.

I am on vacation: a longed for, carefree, pleasure-filled reward for the hard working servant of society, you envision. Ah, but my friend, you forget: this is Vietnam!

I had planned to start my vacation on Thursday, June 8, because there is a flight on Mondays and Thursdays from NhaTrang to BaoLoc. I was going to visit a friend who is work-ing there with IVS. Next I planned to visit our VNCS unit in Quang Ngai. Then I planned to go on to BanMeThuot and finally end up in Saigon for a few days before returning home. Trying to be a considerate guest, I wrote letters to the friends in all of these places advising them approximately when I expected to arrive, trusting it would be all right with them.

Then the frustrations began! Due to military activity, the VNCS administration restricted travel in I Corps to strictly business travel. Quang Ngai is in I Corps and vacation can hardly be considered business travel. Scratch one stop and write one letter of regrets. The timing was perfect for they hadn't yet received my letter of request.

The big day arrived and with only about four hours left after packing, I was ready. Our mechanic, who also serves as chauffeur to the airport, checked on my flight about four hours before flight time to confirm my reservation which had been placed five days before. I wasn't on the passenger list! The office was "very sorry" for its mistake and listed me on the plane for BaoLoc the next day.

Unfortunately they forgot to mention that whereas the plane for BaoLoc on Thursday left at two p.m. the one on Friday left at 8:30 a.m. We arrived to check on it just as it was taxiing down the runway!

NhaTrang is a lovely place to vacation, but I work there and that is a "horse of a different color." Nevertheless, I tried to make the best of those two days of my precious, long-anticipated vacation. So I spent most of the time by myself, sunning or swimming.

Since I was to be in Saigon Sunday night for a farewell dinner for our assistant director and his wife, I decided to change my vacation plans all around and go to Saigon first, visiting the other places on the way back. So off I went to Saigon, and that part of the trip went uneventfully and exactly as planned. After four days in Saigon, I headed for BanMeThuot.

BanMeThuot is a lovely little town in the central highlands of the country. Like the town of Pleiku about which I have previously written, BanMeThuot lies surrounded by territory inhabited mainly by the Montagnard or tribes' people. Many of the tribes surrounding BanMeThuot are different from those at Pleiku but the area appears much the same: a beautiful combination of densely wooded areas with lush green rolling cultivated fields of red clay soil. Anyway that's what it looked like from the air.

When the plane landed, all that was to be seen was a red clay landing strip, a quonset hut surrounded by military vehicles of various kinds, and a sleepy little terminal building bearing an inscription in Vietnamese. But there was no indication of the word *BanMeThuot* or any reasonable facsimile thereof that I could see!

I got off the plane because this was the first stop out of Saigon and the schedule said the first stop would be BanMeThuot. After a noble attempt to find out where I was by asking people in the terminal building (in Vietnamese, of course), I gave up. I headed instead for the quonset hut in hopes of finding some "round eyes." Ten minutes later I was on my way in to BanMeThuot with a USAID nurse who happened to be at the airport. She helped me confirm my flight for the coming week and left me directly at the door of the home of the missionaries with whom I planned to stay. I never would have found them on my own because they live in the midst of a tribes' village on the opposite side of town. Her kindness renewed my courage to continue my travels in this pit-filled paradise.

The day of my arrival in BanMeThuot there began a new frustration. I mention it briefly here because it is so common and so frustrating, although not usually serious. I contracted what has at various times been termed the "Hanoi hops" or the "G.I. trots" (in South America, it is termed "Montezuma's revenge.") In simple layman's terms, it is diarrhea.

It does something to the enthusiasm of a vacation stay in a scenic spot when about the only sights that can be glimpsed are the glories between one's bedroom door and the outhouse. But thanks to a wonderful invention, consisting of a weak combination of opiates creatively named diarrhea tablets, in about twenty-four hours I was able to enjoy the beauties of BanMeThuot farther than ten feet from my door.

Walks through the nearby villages were interesting and a picnic in a lovely and restful place several kilometers out of town was enjoyable. Of course I regret not seeing any of the tigers and elephants that supposedly roam wild not far outside the city.

After four days, fortified with another diarrhea tablet, I picked up my suitcase and bravely set out for BaoLoc. I readily admit, dear reader, that I had not written my friend there of my forced change in vacation plans. I assure you it was not due to thoughtlessness but because it took my first letter exactly twenty days to reach its destination less than three hundred kilometers from where it was sent. So I knew it was useless to try. Still it never occurred to me that . . . but I mustn't get ahead of my story.

For half an hour we flew over beautiful, lush, green jungles, through clouds, sun, a little rain and a little wind. Then we dropped straight down in two tight circles, took a bounce off of an incredibly rough air strip and shuddered to a stop in the middle of a big red clay field without a terminal or even a quonset hut. There was nothing, in fact, except three cars. This was BaoLoc!

While I was pondering on the best way to get a ride into town, I saw my suitcase disappearing towards a jeep. Before I reached the same jeep I had had three offers of rides into town!

Asking the driver of the jeep about my friend, I discovered he knew him. Then after answering my questions, they fired off one of their own: "Are you wife of Mr. Bruce?"

"No," I explained, "only an old friend."

"Oh", said one, "you know I never speak English with American woman before."

"Well," I said bravely, "we speak almost the same language as the men." And then the picture began to get clearer and I wondered: Mary Sue, what have you gotten yourself into?

Arriving at the USAID office, the final frustrating blow settled firmly down on my aching head. Since I had not arrived the week before when I had said that I might, my friend had left for Saigon on business and would not be back for at least two days. I sighed as I listened to the plane on which I had just arrived circling overhead as it gained altitude to go on to NhaTrang. The next plane out doesn't go for three days.

So, tonight, I sit in a strange house in a strange place, three hundred kilometers from home in VC infested jungle. I am playing cards with three strangers, who work for USAID, around a table on which a pistol has been carefully laid. It is not there for decoration I have been informed. We sit waiting for the artillery across the street to begin its nightly harrassment of the VC. This, I repeat, is vacationing in Vietnam. I do hope my friend gets home tomorrow!

I've probably convinced you that there are frustrations in the business of travel in Vietnam sufficient to make me long for a sinkful of dirty dishes or charge nurse duties in a stateside hospital. Let me add a few of the other less acute but nonetheless irritating varieties of this "spicy" life.

Traffic and Driving. The roads, once good, have suffered grievously from the years of military occupation. In the less populated areas, some have been blown up by the VC and in towns like NhaTrang they have been demolished by the heavy military traffic. Chuck holes tend to slow one's trip. The holes are big enough to break an axle and in rainy season become swimming pools for the neighborhood kids. Traffic moves slowly but not slowly enough. It is composed of pedestrians, bicycles, motor scooters of every description and speed, three-wheeled Lambretta scooters, private cars, jeeps, three-quarter ton to 'deuce'n a half' army trucks and, in some places, armored personnel carriers.

Wheels, the bigger the better, are a status symbol and are driven accordingly by the Vietnamese, American, or Korean behind them. The net result is something like an Indianapolis 500 on an obstacle course, and the inevitable clashes occur. An angry purple scar around my left eye bears silent testimony to one of these clashes. The above comments apply to NhaTrang. Saigon is worse!

Shopping. Bargaining over price is a Vietnamese business tradition and it was months before I learned my Vietnamese numbers well enough to be able to hold my own in this cagey sport. The clever Vietnamese, however, now are beginning to wise up to the American fixed price system and, because "rich" and "American" are synonyms in their language, they often will not budge from their first astronomical bid any more.

Luckily there are many shops operated by Chinese or Indian merchants who are generally better businessmen than the Vietnamese. So it is possible to keep oneself supplied with necessities. An additional factor complicating life for the poorer Vietnamese, especially, is inflation. Their motto must be: Buy now for tomorrow you can't afford it. The price of rice has gone up around two hundred percent in the past five years.

The Outside World. The only daily papers I know of in the country are the *Stars and Stripes* and the *Saigon Post,* neither of which is able to give a complete or objective view of news of Vietnam. Asia editions of *Time, Life,* and *Newsweek* are available but are often several weeks old.

Such are some of the frustrations of free time for the volunteer in Vietnam. But, to paraphrase scripture a bit, "With every frustration the Lord provides us means to meet it." With our present work load we have little free time to worry about let alone the frustrations it entails.

Thanks to all of you for letters, remembrances, and prayers.

11

In Reflection

Newsweek
February 27, 1967

Crooks in Toyland

Ex-GI's who served around the racket-ridden port of Manila in the last months of World War II would feel right at home in present-day Saigon. With everything from champagne to the tools of war pouring across its fetid quays at the rate of 4 million tons a year, Saigon currently boasts the world's most numerous and enterprising fraternity of harbor thieves.

By conservative estimate, Saigon's harbor thieves get away with at least 10 per cent of all goods coming into the port. (On easily portable items such as fountain pens and hand tools, loss by theft soars as high as 70 per cent.) . . . .

Last week, in an attempt to choke off the thievery, the government of Premier Nguyen Cao Ky dispatched fresh swarms of tough, sharp-eyed cops into the port area. "This," said a longshoreman a bit sadly, "may mean the end of the individual thief. But, of course, those who have the capital to buy crooked officials and fake papers will survive."

June 29, 1967
NhaTrang

Dear Folks,

Oh, Daddy, your letters have been breaths of spring to me. But when I read them I hope that you are not expecting too much of me. You may be very disappointed. I want to be able to do so much more than I am but, being realistic about myself, it will be a major accomplishment if I just get through these two years with my sanity largely intact. I will feel as if I've accomplished something if I survive.

In these past weeks and months both internal and external circumstances have turned me to an honest attempt at systematic meditation, prayer time, and study of the New Testament. The New English Bible opened up some new understandings to me; the meditation gives me some new insights into myself. But with few exceptions the prayers for strength to do better and be able to be more loving than I am seem to go unanswered. I'm not sure why but that's the way it seems, day after day.

July 13, 1967
NhaTrang

Dear Folks,

Day off again and before I get engrossed in one of several activities I have on the schedule for today, I'll drop you a note. I'm happy to report that I have gained eight pounds in the last three weeks since I got back from vacation. At that time I felt about as lousy as I can remember feeling for a long time. I weighed 105 pounds and my blood pressure was around 80/60 which was causing me frequent dizzy spells.

So, on Doc's advice, I decided to pamper myself a little. I've been trying to eat about five or six times a day, taking a short siesta after lunch almost every day, and I'm trying not to worry so much. It seems to be helping. I feel much better.

In the meantime, I got my hair cut off short the way I like it and made myself a new, bright red dress. The more conservative Mennonites here do not approve of such a gaudy color. One of them said to me, "You know what kind of woman wears a red dress in Vietnam, don't you?" I replied, "Yes, but if people can't tell by looking that I'm not that kind of woman then they've got more problems than I do!"

I also made a new blouse to wear with my satin Vietnamese pants. It's like a tunic, sleeveless with a belt. It's made out of two Indian silk scarves and is very comfortable. The folks here laugh at that, too, but I don't care. The new clothes raised my spirits. I'm also getting back to studying and writing lectures, this time in microbiology, and I love that.

So, all in all, I'm feeling better than I have for a while. Those books and articles they write on culture shock and acculturation should be able to warn a person. However, I think you have to experience it to believe it. The articles about culture shock mention the difficulties of getting used to different customs, people, and language. They don't mention much about climate changes, strange diseases, overwork and difficulty with coworkers. Those are as difficult as the other adjustments.

The biggest thing I'm learning lately is simply to slow down, physically and mentally. Much of my feverish activity and worrying doesn't do anybody any good and just wears me to a frazzle. There's really no merit in ruining my health in foreign service unless it's necessary. So I've decided to wait till it's necessary and in the meantime eat, drink, and relax!

We've finally moved into the new house in full force. The doctor and his wife and one of the other nurses live in the house, and I have a room in the servant's quarters out behind the house. There may be some pictures of the house on one of these rolls of film.

It's very nice except that we were without water for about two months because the old pump they tried to use kept blowing fuses. Finally, two days ago a new pump was purchased and installed and now we have all the water we want right at our fingertips. So yesterday the pump over at the other house and the hospital gave up the ghost. Now everybody has to come over here to get water. Such a nuisance.

One of the nurses just got back from her out-of-country vacation to Cambodia, Thailand, and Malaysia for two weeks. I didn't know until about a month ago that we Brethren volunteers are also allowed to take an out-of-country vacation if we want to. I hadn't planned on it so I guess I'll just stop at a few of these places on my way home.

We had a little excitement around here last weekend. The Christian and Missionary Alliance organization in New York sent a new missionary couple to Vietnam to establish a Christian Serviceman's Center in Saigon. The wife was eight months pregnant with their first child. The mission headquarters assured her that she could be delivered in a military hospital.

Well, that is definitely not the case and she could not be delivered in a Vietnamese Province Hospital because she is an American. I'm sure they did quite a bit of praying about the time they found this out, because her doctor in the States had predicted she would have difficulties with the delivery. She has such a small pelvic outlet and both she and her husband are big people. So the Christian and Missionary Alliance folks in Saigon sent her here.

Of course we said we would deliver her. Then Doc discovered that she had gained almost thirty pounds with this pregnancy. So, when she came down to the hospital last Saturday morning with her husband, we were ready for some complications. She had been having labor pains for about four hours already and had a good labor. By eight p.m. she was completely dilated but, by that time, Doc suspected yet one more complication so he ordered an x-ray.

Our new x-ray machine, for which we have waited so long and impatiently, has now been in operation for about two weeks and we have taken 120 films. The technician which we had trained at the Province Hospital in NhaTrang is doing excellently and his films are coming out better than those we used to get taken at Province Hospital. On this particular night it was a real blessing to have the x-ray so close.

The x-ray confirmed Doc's suspicions: it was a breech presentation! So he got out all the obstetric books, laid them out on the cupboards in the nurses station and started reading, wandering down the line from one to another. The other doctor jumped on the scooter and roared off to Eighth Field Military Hospital in NhaTrang to plead for the possibility of admission for a C-section if we absolutely couldn't deliver her.

By ten p.m. she was pushing well and we could see a little buttocks. Doc read one more book, asked one of the nurses if the forceps were sterilized and decided we would deliver her ourselves. The other doctor got back in time to scrub and helped lay an anesthetic block.

By that time she was pushing like an oldtimer and thinking of nothing else. In fact, we were all so engrossed in helping her that we forgot to give her the Trilene gas we had promised her to help take the edge off the discomfort. At 10:30 p.m. Doc did a large episiotomy to prevent tearing of the maternal tissues and ten minutes later, with a mighty heave, she pushed the buttocks of the baby out without even needing forceps.

She was so happy and proud and we were mighty relieved. We were even more relieved that they had no trouble delivering the head and they had a beautiful little girl of seven pounds, eight ounces. We are all very happy and thankful that things worked out so well.

Well, more news another time. I must get to my books and do a little studying. The idea that I teach microbiology is ludicrous enough even if I had all sorts of reference books. But without any . . . it boggles my imagination. But I'm having fun trying.

July 24, 1967
NhaTrang

Dear Folks,
Yesterday afternoon, Sunday, we drove down to Cam Ranh Bay to visit some missionary friends who used to work in NhaTrang. They're leaving for furlough in the States and it was our last chance to say good-by. This is the first time I've made the trip and it is the longest trip I've yet made in this country by land transportation. It took about an hour and a half one way but check your map for the distance. Part of the reason it took so long is the very poor condition of the roads; I doubt if it's farther than sixty miles.

The roads may be terrible but the scenery was lovely. Rice fields are being cultivated just now and they are that lovely indescribable green color that I shall always associate with Vietnam. Cam Ranh itself isn't much to look at—all military establishment—but it was good to see our friends again. It was just like a Sunday afternoon back home.

August 3, 1967
NhaTrang

Dear Folks,

The scrapbooks you sent finally arrived. By this time I suppose you also know what happened. I thought I had told Carl to tell the serviceman whose APO number I used that I was expecting some packages. I guess I forgot. When they arrived, he had no idea whose they were. Assuming they were for him, he began to use them in teaching his English classes. Finally, I guess, he wrote to you and you answered and explained. So last night he sent them out here to me. Thank-you—and the children who made the books—very much.

I have put a large, brightly colored box in the nurses' station right behind my desk. I put a few of those scrapbooks and a stack of *National Geographics* in this box. That way the children who are constantly running around the hospital can come and help themselves. Of course the books will gradually disappear but that cannot be prevented except by locking them up. We are planning to collect a few books on health, general reading, religion, and other topics and start a small lending library for the adults, those who can read. The others enjoy the picture books with the children.

Time is passing incredibly fast. My term is now seventeen months down and seven to go. I'm answering letters with postmarks in March and it seems like last month that I got them! Spare time just isn't what it used to be. I'm teaching English again; this time to three Catholic nuns on Wednesday evenings.

I'm still trying to write microbiology lectures but, thank goodness, the anatomy and physiology lectures are all written. Also, for the past two weeks, I've been puttering around in the lab to see what I could get into.

To call it a lab is flattering it. It is in the corner of one of the doctor's offices and is stocked with very few reagents, most of them three years old. There is almost no glassware. Last week I spent an afternoon in at Eighth Field Military Hospital in NhaTrang literally begging for a set of gram stain reagents from them. It was worth the effort, however, because last night I finally got a good gram stain—of my own throat!

Of course we don't have any stock cultures or culture media. So I have taken all smears from fresh specimens. Most of the hospitalized patients have been on antibiotics long enough to kill all the infecting bacteria, however, so I was not getting good results from smears taken from them. I hope to make a small set of study slides which we can use in studying microbiology this fall. It is entailing more work than I had anticipated though.

I was glad for the two copies of *Between the Lines* you sent and for the article concerning the riots in Detroit. We don't get too much coverage of this kind of news over here but perhaps the newest issues of *Time* and *Newsweek* will have something to say about it. In their Asian editions, however, they seem to be very careful what they say and how they report it.

The *Stars and Stripes*, the Armed Forces newspaper, has had very little coverage of it at all. Of course we know a little about those riots (as do all the servicemen serving in this country) but it might be a shock to read about it in print. It's a blow to our idealistic dreams of what home is and it gives a sort of "why go home?" feeling. It also gives some a feeling of "why fight here?" The other day I heard a serviceman say, "Yes, sir. I'm with the United States Army, the best in the world: fighting on the battlefronts of the world, Vietnam and Detroit!"

August 10, 1967
NhaTrang

Dear Folks,
Another weekly note, and before I forget to tell you, I gave your address to one of our military chaplain friends. He will be going home in about five days to his family in Columbus, Ohio and he offered to call you if he could to tell you how I'm getting along. I asked him to reverse the charges but he probably won't. He conducted the chapel services at the military chapel where we used to play the organ. He's a good man and anything but a "God bless our boys" Army chaplain (but don't tell him I said so!)

Last Sunday five of us drove up to Ninh Hoa and even a little north of there. It's a lovely drive through a peaceful countryside of fishing villages and rice fields. Military traffic (both American and Korean) on the road is tremendous and the surface of the road is very bad as a result. But it is passable.

At one point, where we stopped to take pictures, we actually saw a train running. The White Horse Division of the Korean Army was sent here from Korea expressly for the task of securing roads and railroads around NhaTrang and Ninh Hoa. So, thanks to them, we can now drive to Ninh Hoa in perfect safety and the trains are running again from DaLat to Phan Rang. It was the first train I had seen in eighteen months because absolutely no trains can run in and out of Saigon.

On the way home, a slight drizzle turned the road rather slick. We saw a bus suddenly come swerving and careening down the road toward us. Thinking he might hit us we pulled off the road and stopped. Then we saw why he swerved. A bicycle carrying two boys had turned out in front of him. In swerving to miss it he had bumped it just hard enough to knock the boy off the back.

We went back to see if we could help, of course, and a crowd began to gather from nowhere. Doc decided from the angle of the left hand and wrist that it was probably broken. We made a splint for it from a piece of cardboard and an ace bandage which one of our nurses unwrapped from her broken foot.

He had various other lacerations and we decided that he needed to be cleaned up, checked, and x-rayed. We had told the people who we were so the boy would know that Doc would not harm him, and almost all the people in the crowd knew where our hospital was. We were just a few kilometers south of Ninh Hoa, about thirty kilometers from home, so we offered to take the boy to the hospital at Ninh Hoa thinking it would be closer to his home.

Then one man in the crowd, speaking in English, said, "Could you take him with you in your car back to your hospital?" So I asked the boy in Vietnamese where he wanted to go and he also said he wanted to go with us back to our little clinic. In the background I could hear many voices in the crowd (not knowing that some of us could understand) commenting favorably about Chan-Y-Vien Tin-Lanh. They knew where it was and many had had friends and relatives treated there. We were truly amazed that such fame had spread thirty kilometers from our humble establishment. It did us all good in our hearts!

We finally decided to do something about our prolific pup! Talofa Lava (Polynesian for "Dear One" or something) is our smaller dog. She actually belongs to Marcy and is a cute little thing, but she seems to have a litter of pups three or four times a year. The patients don't mind because "puppy meat" *pho* (soup) is quite a delicacy but we're getting tired of it.

So we began to feed Talofa the birth control pills we had in the clinic which we couldn't use on our human patients. (Most of our patients would not have calenders or any means to reliably keep up with the three-week-on-one-week-off schedule which birth control pills require. Besides, with husbands and sons being killed off in the war, who needs birth control pills to prevent overpopulation?)

Anyway, afraid we might run out of a supply of birth control pills, we decided we'd better do a tubal ligation ("tying the tubes") on Talofa so she would be permanently retired from motherhood. On the appointed day, after our usual morning staff devotional period at the clinic, we slipped her a sedative in a meat ball. Then, after our human surgery schedule was completed, we carried the sleepy little brown mass into the operating room. Unfortunately, by this time, the sedative was beginning to wear off; and our doctors, accustomed to human arms instead of canine paws, could not find a vein into which to give anesthesia. Marcy could not stand the thought of them cutting her dear pup open without anesthetic. And Talofa herself greeted all this attention with continual and pitiful howling!

The hospital and clinic patients and their family members clustered around outside the doors and windows of the operating room in curious groups wondering, no doubt, what kind of an evil spirit the American doctors and nurses were exorcising now. In desperation, we gave up our efforts at surgical sterilization of our prolific pooch. We had to admit defeat; and she marched gratefully and unsteadily out of the operating room with her innards intact. No doubt we'll have another batch of pups in a few months.

August 17, 1967
NhaTrang

Dear Sisters All,

Letter writing to you all seems to have degenerated into a semiannual occurrence. I hasten to assure you that that is in inverse proportion to the frequency with which you are in my thoughts. Already August is more than half finished and I honestly can't remember where July went. This year is a great contrast to last year which seemed to crawl along its way. Last July was about sixty days long and every one of them was blistering hot. It's still hot but the days don't last long enough to mind the heat so much.

Thinking back to one year ago reminds me of all the changes that have come about here since then. Most of them mark progress, I think.

Our Vietnamese staff has increased by nearly half. The TB hospital built last "winter" now houses thirty patients more than we previously had space for. The x-ray machine has been operating for about two months, more than three hundred films have been taken already, and a TB immunization program has begun. Hospital admissions have increased by two hundred more than they were last year at this time. I think this reflects patients coming in, getting better treatment, and getting discharged earlier so that additional admissions can be made. We're having occasional health education classes for the clinic patients while they wait and the surgery load is now so heavy that we have to operate three days a week instead of two.

In addition to all of this, we have big plans for the future. Plans for the nursing school are already taking shape. There's a possibility of our conducting roving TB and health education clinics. We're planning to improve our laboratory facilities and perhaps build another TB hospital.

Sounds like I'm bragging, doesn't it? I am a little except that I have had very little to do with instituting any of these accomplishments. I have to content myself with progress in the realms of bath schedules, temperatures, accuracy in giving medicines and, millimeter by millimeter, scratching away at the accumulated and everpresent dirt of this place. In that there is little progress! Incidentally, however, there's also been a little progress in my state of mind.

Before I forget it, I must commend to you a book, *Ten Vietnamese* by Susan Sheehan. She writes it, she says, about the ninety-five percent of people that don't count. Although she was not writing about our patients here, she might have been. It gives a better description of some of the types of people we treat than any news release, history, or political tract ever could. You can read it in about five or six hours.

The other day in *Stars and Stripes,* the Armed Forces newspaper, of all places, there was an article reporting the work of a Democratic Representative from New York and his investigation of gross waste in military spending. One example he gave was a metal rod which listed for 50 cents apiece. The U.S. military had paid $25.55 each.

He went on to say that the piece was listed as "precision shafting." For once, he said, the American taxpayer had gotten exactly what he had paid for! He cited other examples and this type of thing goes on all the time on both sides of the Pacific. Most of that extra money ends up in pockets that are already too well lined.

The American press, for the most part, assists this practice by its silence. They create inch and a half headlines about how demonstrators, picketers, and draft card burners are prolonging this insanity of war. But the press ignores the thousands of businessmen buying new Cadillacs every year on the padding from big defense contracts. Those same businessmen support lobbies in Washington to pressure the Congressmen for increased expenditures to pursue this "holy war" against Communism. The only conflict they're really interested in is the struggle to get more money into their pockets. I'm sick and tired of the whole mess but I don't think coming home will help this feeling at all. It seems that so much of the stupidity that escalates the conflict on this side of the Pacific generates on that side of the ocean and is then exported a safe distance from those responsible. Reading back over that, perhaps you'd better be careful about quoting me on this. Somebody might cancel my passport!

Well, enough of my ramblings for this time. Not all is business and politics, I assure you. I'm just recovering from a sunburn from last Sunday afternoon's boating and swimming off a lovely island out in the harbor.

August 25, 1967
NhaTrang

Dear Folks,

Just a quick note a day late before I begin typing lectures. I finally got the course and the tests for it all written. Now I have to type out about three or four copies of it: one for me, one for a translator, one for the nurse director, and one for the Ministry of Health. It's rather long so I'll probably have to cut some of it out, but at least it's finished. Now all I have to do is make some teaching aids. Progress towards the school isn't moving too fast but the ground is now cleared for the dormitory-classroom building and we know of three students.

It's raining today almost as if it were rainy season and we only had sixty-two patients in clinic this morning. But it's only August and the real rains shouldn't come until about the first of October. Mind you I'm not complaining because it's so much cooler when it rains. Besides that it's rather pretty and not at all depressing to me to see the grass get green again and see the sea turn to a gray blue rainy color.

The doctor and his wife have gone for a week of vacation to visit our VNCS unit at Di Linh and a missionary family from Saigon is staying here for their vacation. Carl leaves for the States in about a week or so as his term is finished. He's flying to Singapore, picking up a motorcycle, and cycling through as much of Asia, the Middle East, and Europe as he can before he embarks by ship from Portugal to home. His replacement, Jim Bowman, is staying here this week learning the ropes of the job.

One of our nurses is vacationing in Hue and another VNCS family from Saigon will be coming to spend the weekend with us. Early next week there are some Wycliffe missionaries coming to their summer house on our compound here. We feel a little like a resort hotel!

Well, I must get on with typing lectures. More news later.

August 31, 1967
NhaTrang

Dear Folks,

How envious I am of your going to Austria. I should talk, shouldn't I? If you'd only wait about five months I'd join you in Vienna. Better yet, why don't you spend about $500 apiece more and come to Saigon and NhaTrang and visit me? You'd love it here. At least you would, Daddy. Mother, you'd have as many problems as I do, from diarrhea to depression. This place isn't much of a tourist attraction, especially right now before elections with the VC bombing the polling places. But maybe you could get yourselves appointed a Brethren Service fact-finding team to Asia and get your expenses paid for you!

Somewhere among my slides is a picture of a Korean couple. He is in Army uniform and she is in a beautiful blue native Korean dress, distinctly different from the Vietnamese *ao dai*. If you can find the picture, please get a print made and send it to me so I can give it to them for Christmas. He was the Protestant chaplain at the Korean camp near us here and his wife was a nurse at the hospital. They have since gone back to Korea but they left me a beautiful souvenir and I promised to send them a Christmas card.

September 7, 1967
NhaTrang

Dear folks,

Such a week this has been. Carl, our dear Paxman, left yesterday to go to Saigon for three days. Then he will go on to the States via Asia and Europe on a motorcycle he will pick up in Singapore. Naturally all of his friends wanted to say good-by so he has only eaten about three meals at home in the past two weeks. Some of the invitations included us, too. We've all been filled up on *chay do,* a delicious fried meat roll (meat filling wrapped in rice paper), which is often served to company.

Sunday we had an open house and informal tea to which we invited his Vietnamese and American friends. About fifty people came. Tuesday afternoon the hospital board gave a more formal tea for the hospital staff. Yesterday evening twelve of us took him to the plane and shed a few tears as he took off for home.

The article you sent reporting on the translation of the New Testament for the Koho tribespeople was very interesting. It was even more interesting because I know many of the people pictured and mentioned in the article.

September 14, 1967
Nha Trang

Dear Folks,

Another week come and gone, and where to? It has been a busy one for us. Judy Aaker, the wife of the VNCS director had her first baby here yesterday. She had come up from Saigon about two weeks ago to wait. Then last Sunday evening she began to have some contractions which continued through Monday and Tuesday. Tuesday night they got harder so the three of us—she, her husband, and I—sat up all night timing them. Still no baby. So, on two hours of sleep, I went back to work. Finally, at 4:30 p.m. Wednesday, a seven pound, seven ounce boy appeared on the scene. Everyone was relieved that things went well.

Our chief interpreter, Co Tranh Thi Thanh, is coming to the States to enroll at Eastern Mennonite College for the second semester of this year. I do not know yet when this term starts exactly. If it is not too long before my term of service ends, I will plan to leave a little early and travel home with her. This would help us both. It would eliminate all sightseeing on my way home but I would have good company. I'll let you know what I decide.

12

In Coming Home

Newsweek
May 9, 1966

Diary Of A Soldier

(Though there are more than 25,000 North Vietnamese regulars now fighting in South Vietnam, so little information of a personal nature is available about them that they have remained a faceless enemy. Recently, however, NEWSWEEK's Francois Sully came into possession of the diary of a young North Vietnamese named Nguyen Quang Le, a radio operator in an artillery unit. In artless but vivid language, Le's diary describes his parting with his family a year ago, and the tedium and travail of the long trek south across the 17th parallel into battle. Some excerpts:)

MAY 1, 1965: Today is farewell day. Departure takes place in a few hours. Meanwhile, Ngoan [his wife] sews a book bag for me. Since my return, there have been constant visitors. The village people are indeed very kind. In the dark of the night or under pelting rain like tonight, they come to see us in large numbers. Not knowing what I have to do yet, they urge me to do my best in killing the enemy. I find our people highly aware of the situation and they feel a deep anti-Americanism. Mrs. Phu [a neighbor] behaved insipidly. She wept bitterly and this shocked my family.

(After joining his unit, Le proceeds by truck to Hanoi where he notes a shortage of rice. From there, he travels by train to his base camp at Thai Nguyen.)

MAY 11: It's hard to sleep tonight. I don't mind who has to go to south Vietnam first. All my worry centers around the day of reunification and whether I will come back unscathed. How will the family be then? . . . Ngoan will be a bit older, but she remains the wife who receives all my love. Even if Ngoan has a love child, I will tolerate her . . . Such thoughts assault my mind, and I toss and toss, spending a wakeful night.

MAY 24: This morning, political study. Twelve men in my unit head for south Vietnam. Yesterday, the political commissar read out the list of names and I was surprised that my name was not mentioned. Next time, then . . . . (After another ten days of routine military training and political indoctrination, Le finally gets his orders to proceed to the town of Thanh Hoa, 60 miles south of Hanoi in North Vietnam's Military Zone IV.)

JUNE 11: Things look different in the war zone; troops are more appreciated here. At the bus station, our troops chat with the girls in high spirits. The war is felt more acutely in this zone. People work at night. Cars run without headlights and are heavily camouflaged. Even the bicycles are camouflaged.

JUNE 12: Each step brings us closer to war. Each step shows us more clearly the crimes of the U.S. invaders. Even small bridges that span National Highway One get bombed. At 8 p.m. we stop at a communications post on the roadside, I want to boil some water, but enemy aircraft whir overhead and we must drink half-boiled water. It rains persistently and we get drenched in this nagging rain during the night.

JUNE 13: Today we enjoyed only one meal because of the shortage of rice. We feel dog tired as we walk in the night. Over a stretch of 25 to 30 miles, the crimes of the U.S. imperialists are scattered here and there. The pine forest is charred by U.S. rockets. The bridges are blasted by U.S. bombs, the railroads melted and the houses burned. This fans the flames of hate in everyone. . . .

(Toward the middle of August, Le prepares for the final stage of his journey into South Vietnam. He is inoculated against various diseases and gets his hair cut. Off duty he rereads "The Way the Steel is Tempered" by North Vietnam's Defense Minister Gen. Vo Nguyen Giap, and notes "there are passages that truly drive me to tears." In late September, the move begins in earnest and Le has little time to write in his diary except to list the names of the towns his unit passes through as it proceeds south. The months of November and December are left blank as Le makes the dangerous crossing of the 17th parallel into the Ben Hai River Delta area near the town of Quang Tri.) . . . .

JAN. 25: After lunch, we get orders for an urgent operation.

JAN. 26: Tonight, melancholy. I think of nothing.

FEB. 6: I stay awake all night because of the cursed boil on my shoulder.

FEB. 18: Yesterday evening, I had the mission shown to me on the map.

FEB. 20: After lunch my section heads for Kb [an abbreviation for a place name]. We get lost. To lose one's way is disturbing. No liaison agents show us the way. Yet I feel happy, particularly when at nightfall troops pour out from the forest like so many ants. But when the night comes and all-night operations take place on the sand hills, my knees sag. After 3 a.m., the first unit opens fire. I stay awake all night.

FEB. 22: The building of installations goes on in preparation for fighting.

(So ends the last entry in the diary of Nguyen Quang Le. Weeks later, when an enemy defector turned himself over to South Vietnamese authorities, Le's diary was found in his possession. On the rumpled cover of the diary were the dark stains of dried blood.)

September 26, 1967
Brookville, Ohio, USA

Dear Friends,

What a blessing it is that God never consults us before making plans for us nor even gives us a glimpse beforehand of what is in store. I, for one, would lose days fretting and worrying about something over which I had no control whatsoever, like last week. Let me explain.

A week ago yesterday was Trung-Thu, the second most important festival of the lunar year. It is the children's festival in midautumn and what a lovely celebration they have for it at the orphanage. Just as it gets dark the children began lighting the candles inside their variously shaped, transparent, colored paper "japanese" lanterns. The children of our Vietnamese staff saw to it that the doctor's baby was well supplied. He had three lanterns before the day arrived!

About 7:30 in the evening a great parade began, led by a fearsome looking six-legged dragon and his papier-maché-headed trainer. Up and down the orphanage lane they led all the children who were carrying their lighted lanterns. There were about two hundred orphans plus an assortment of neighborhood children. To the accompaniment of a drum and tambourines they "take a trip to the moon" to thank him for his help in making the crops grow. It's a lovely sight and a very happy time for the children who are kept well supplied with candies and *banh Trung-Thu,* a special kind of cake for the occasion.

After several trips up and down the lane, we all retired to the school auditorium and were entertained by the orphanage residents, as each little living unit presented some entertainment for the whole group. There were funny skits, often written by the children themselves; graceful dances by lovely little girls; vocal solos and, of course, first and last, a dance by the dragon and his trainer.

Every year the holiday is held at the full moon of the mid-autumn month and the walk home by the sea is as beautiful a part of the celebration as the parade. This year a couple of our Vietnamese friends invited us to a moonlight picnic by the sea to share their *Trung-Thu* cake. We had a lovely time. That was on Monday.

Wednesday morning, just two days later, the personnel director of Vietnam Christian Service arrived in NhaTrang from Saigon and called for a unit meeting within five minutes after he arrived. We knew the news was important if he called us from our work but we were not prepared for what he told us.

Our young Mennonite Paxman, Carl, had left us just two weeks before for Singapore to buy a motorcycle on which to cycle home through Asia and Europe. He had been killed in Singapore in a traffic accident four days before but the news had not yet reached us.

Not knowing this young man, you cannot fully appreciate the effect this shock had on us who had worked with him for a year and a half or more. He was one of the handsomest and most charming people I have ever known and was refreshingly unconscious of these gifts. He had a boyish honesty about himself and his faith and a man's ability to get a job done. He was loved by more people in his twenty-three years than most people are in a lifetime. At that time he was closer to the hearts of every person in the unit than their own families because we had lived and worked with him so recently. We notified the Vietnamese staff immediately and went about carrying the sad news to some of the neighbors who had know him especially well.

Arriving home, the VNCS staffer who had brought us the news asked for a few more minutes of my time before I returned to work. He then showed me a telegram the Saigon office had received from my family: "Father seriously ill. Family wishes her return."

There was no choice. I told him to get plane tickets for both of us to Saigon as soon as possible and I'd be ready to leave by Thursday morning. Then I went to my room. I did something I had not done for a long, long time. I knelt beside my bed, bowed my head on my folded hands and simply said, "Help, Lord!" That was probably the most desperate prayer I have ever prayed.

The answer seemed to come in an almost audible voice: "Yes. Get up now. You have much to do." There was a knock on the door and I got up to answer it. It was one of our nurses who had come to help me. In one short afternoon she and I packed all of my things completely. I was able also to visit various friends to tell them I had to leave. We all conferred with the minister of the nearby Vietnamese Protestant church about a memorial service for Carl. This service was planned completely in about three hours!

At 7:30 that night we gathered in the nearby church for a service of remembrance for Carl and his family. There must have been nearly sixty of our Vietnamese and American missionary friends who joined us in the church. The building was illuminated only by candles and one kerosene lantern suspended from the ceiling because the church is not adequately wired for the use of electricity at night.

The service was relatively short, about an hour, and entirely in Vietnamese except for a short biography of our young friend that Doc read in English which was, then, translated for the congregation. The rest of us in the unit tried to sing a hymn which was a favorite of Carl's, "Lift Your Glad Voices." We could not get through it because of our grief and the doctor had to read the words of that also. Psalm 91 was read and the choir sang "Jesus, Lover of my Soul."

It was a fitting and lovely tribute to our young friend. One of the nurses commented later that perhaps it was also a new kind of ministry to the Vietnamese for them to see us, "all mighty and powerful Americans" bowed down by the same kind of grief they have all felt at one time or another. They lent us their strength and I had countless assurances of prayers for my father's health and for my safe return home before I left the church.

Thursday morning, friends dropped in by twos and threes to wish me well and give me gifts of remembrance. I didn't try to work, although I suddenly began to realize how much I was going to miss it. I had dessert with some of the Vietnamese staff and, then, lunch with the unit. We ended lunch with a devotional period together which we usually held in the evening after dinner. We read from Psalms and sang together for the last time:

"Lift your glad voices in triumph on high
For Jesus hath risen and man shall not die;
Vain were the terrors that gathered around him
And short the dominion of death and the grave."

How I always enjoyed our singing together!

We were all sad but it was easier for me to leave at this time than at any time previously for I had been enjoying my work so much more this last six or eight months. I knew that, as much as we had irritated each other over the past year and a half together, we were going to miss each other. I had learned from these folks some valuable lessons of faith I would never forget. Most of us would never see each other again but we would remember each other.

The plane left at three p.m. so we left for the airport about two p.m., accompanied by nearly a dozen Vietnamese friends as well as almost the entire unit. Since I was traveling by Air America, we had to drive onto the military base to catch the plane. The guards there are always quite strict about allowing Vietnamese civilians on the base but we decided to try for my sake. As might be expected at a crucial time like this, despite my tear-stained face, the guard was adamant: "No can do. No can do."

So, in a light drizzle from the heavens and a heavy rain down my cheeks, my Vietnamese friends clambered out and we waved good-by as we went through the gate. I arrived at the airport, boarded right on time, but still the rest of the farewell party, following in the other car, had not arrived.

Just as they were loading the last few boxes on our plane, I saw an assortment of people running out to the plane led by one of our nurses. She had seen our Vietnamese friends waiting outside the gate, figured immediately what had happened and had given the guard such a hard time that, in desperation, he finally let the whole group in!

I went back to the door of the plane for another round of handshaking, assurance of prayers, bursts of tears, and farewell speeches in Vietnamese. I now wonder what I said because I really wasn't thinking too clearly and intelligible conversation in Vietnamese always required my full concentration!

Then, we were off. I was not dry-eyed as I watched Hon Chong, the beach, the bridges, and the Buddha slip past below the windows of our plane because part of me was down there. Part of them was with me, never to be lost.

After a day in Saigon and a fast round of good-by visits to several friends there, I found myself on a Pan American Clipper on Saturday, bound for Honolulu via Guam. From there I traveled to Los Angeles and, by way of Chicago, to Dayton. I arrived home almost exactly thirty-one hours after I left Saigon. To everyone's relief and surprise I was still able to walk but, believe me, jet lag is not an imaginary phenomenon!

After a few hours' sleep I visited Daddy in the hospital. He is still in the Intensive Care Unit which limits visiting privileges to one member of the family for five minutes every hour. They had alerted him that I was coming home and he recognized me immediately. He smiled at me, then said, "You really shouldn't have come home, you know!" Nevertheless, I could tell he was glad to see me and his joy made my trip home worth while. On the plane, high in the air just outside of Chicago, I received a strange, calm assurance that he would improve, as indeed he did, and is!

He is suffering from acute pancreatitis and his condition is still critical but he has improved since last week. We have no assurance that he will recover completely and he may not recover at all. But being together again, the family knows that, because of his life with us, our living will go on no matter what happens. And we are ready for whatever will come.

So I will be at home for a little while with Mother, giving her a chance to fatten me up. My weight is only slightly over a hundred pounds but she is doing her culinary best to improve that situation. I may attempt to find a teaching position (I know not where) for the second semester of the present school year. In the lazy meantime I hope to do a bit of traveling if Daddy's condition improves enough to allow it.

In one short week's time I have been uprooted from one home and returned to another. Culture shock, in a milder form, assails me again. It will decrease, I am sure, as it did in Vietnam, when I get caught up in the daily life of the culture and in working with people again. For then I will be reminded, over and over, not of differences but of similarities.

All people everywhere love, hate, laugh when they're happy, eat, sleep, die, like to be listened to, get sick sometimes and are loved by God. War is tragic proof that as humans—and as nations—we have not yet learned that lesson. This past year and a half has convinced me that there must be a better way!

Our prayers for my father's health seem to be answered because his condition is slowly improving. And, for you, my friends, I pray that you may be as richly blessed in your place of service—whether home, shop, here, or far away—as I was in these past eighteen months in Vietnam.